How to DAO

Kickstart an LLC, crypto hedge fund, or charity from your bedroom

Terry Winters

Copyright © 2021 by Terry Winters. All rights reserved.

No part of this book may be reproduced or used in any manner without the prior written permission of the copyright owner, except for the use of brief quotations in a book review.

ISBN: 9798783175374

Important Disclaimer

The information contained in this book does not constitute legal or financial advice and should never be used without first consulting with a financial professional to determine what may be best for your individual needs. None of the content published in this book constitutes a recommendation of a particular cryptocurrency or investment. None of the information provided is intended to advise you personally concerning the nature, potential, value or suitability of any particular cryptocurrency or any other matter, including tax, legal, or investment advice. Always conduct your own due diligence and never invest more than you are willing to lose in a worst-case scenario.

For inquiries, suggestions, or expressions of interest to cooperate, please contact me at:
terrywinters@protonmail.com

Get to know me on Twitter: terrywinters07

ABBREVIATIONS

DAO: decentralized autonomous organization

A DAO is a decentralized organization where all decisions are made through an open and transparent voting process and then recorded and executed on a public blockchain ledger. The organization is also autonomous, meaning that it runs itself without any need for central control.

NFT: non-fungible token

An NFT is a token that cannot be directly interchanged with any other token. This means that a digital collectible such as a CryptoPunks artwork associated with one token is not equal in value to a token associated with another artist's token or even other tokens minted by the same artist. This enables art and other unique assets to be recorded forever on the blockchain and easily verified at any time.

Multi-sig: Multi-signature wallet

A digital wallet that requires multiple signatures to authorize a transaction, as opposed to a single signature. A multi-sig wallet enables groups to divide responsibility for the possession of cryptocurrencies and other digital assets among multiple individuals.

WAGMI: We are gonna make it

Internet parlance typically used in online trading groups to express comradery after good news related to their investment or asset holdings.

TABLE OF CONTENTS

PROLOGUE	5
INTRODUCTION	7
FROM CENTRALIZED TO DECENTRALIZED	17
THE EARLY GENESIS OF DAOS	25
HOW DO DAOS WORK?	31
TYPES OF DAOS	38
BEST PRACTICES IN DAO DESIGN	46
STARTING YOUR OWN JOURNEY	62
HOW TO CREATE A DAO	74
DAO TOOLS	82
THE FUTURE OF DAOS	91
THANK YOU	95
APPENDIX	97
FURTHER RESOURCES	101
FREQUENTLY ASKED QUESTIONS	102

PROLOGUE

It was named "Stay Free" and it was the second item on their quest to own the most iconic collectibles in the NFT space.

What had begun as a private Telegram chat group to buy a commemorative NFT video in the summer was now a powerful organization with its own governance token, treasury, and mission recorded on the Ethereum blockchain.

The group's first NFT acquisition was called x*y=k. Designed by the multidisciplinary-come-NFT artist pplpleasr, the animated video was commissioned for the launch of Uniswap V3 in the summer of 2020 (https://youtu.be/5o1G3UiGTVw). It, too, was put up for sale at a charity auction. The winning bid? A staggering 310 ETH (USD $525,000).

PleasrDAO was already on the hunt for their next acquisition. Over recent days, the DAO had received a swell of internal member contributions—all sent in a cryptocurrency called Ether (ETH)—to their organization's multi-sig (multi-signature) wallet.

The item for sale was an image of Edward Snowden. It was part of a one-of-one NFT collection signed by the NSA whistle-blower himself and with proceeds from the sale earmarked to raise funds for the Freedom of the Press Foundation.

For PleasrDAO, "Stay Free" was a symbol of why building a more decentralized Internet is vital to protecting democracy and it would make for a notable addition to their digital collection.

Buoyed by the financial support of member contributions, the DAO's chat group was decidedly upbeat coming into the auction. Once again, they were confident that they would come out of the auction a winner. But this web of optimism was soon ruptured once the bidding started. Some other bidder was pushing them towards the upper limit of their treasury balance and, amidst the fury of bids, they quickly found themselves on the sidelines. The other party had just submitted a bid in excess of their ceiling limit. With no more funds available, they were unable to make any further bids.

Not giving up, they searched internally for a solution, and then—at the 11th hour—the DAO's people negotiated a loan of USD $2 million from an unnamed member of the organization.

The fresh funds swept into the DAO's Ethereum wallet. With four minutes remaining until the auction ended, a member operating under the pseudonym G Money liaised with another member of the organization to write a custom transaction. In the nascent web 3 era, their multi-sig wallet did not integrate with Foundation—an NFT marketplace that, like their organization, didn't exist 12 months prior.

With time ticking down and only 10 seconds left, three members of the DAO scrambled to click "Accept" to execute the transaction with infinite gas. It would be their last and final bid.

As the three members scrambled to accept the transaction, the rest of the organization watched on from their screens and waited for an update on the state of play. Blow-by-blow updates came flying in.

"The money is in the multi-sig"

"The bid has been sent!"

"We won it!! WAGMI"

PleasrDAO had won their second charity auction. They were now the proud co-owners of a one-of-one NFT and a USD $5 million snapshot of history. Fittingly, "Stay Free" was now owned by a collective digital community—an organization with no headquarters, no papers of incorporation, and no single patron.

1

INTRODUCTION

Every day, we hand our trust over to centralized organizations. But what happens when an organization becomes decentralized, and *what exactly is* a decentralized autonomous organization (DAO)?
Breaking with the bureaucratic weight of centralized organizations, DAOs represent a staggering change in group thinking, action, and decision-making. They exist as a network of self-coordinated participants who act in their own mutual self-interest to architect and implement a system that can realize collective goals and fulfill the mission of the organization—all without a central leader. Indeed, the main idea is to take power away from central authority figures and replace it in the hands of all the individuals who provide the organization with funding, time, and resources. This framework not only reduces overhead costs from the involvement of third parties or middle layers of management but also helps to solve what's known as the *principal-agent problem*.
The principal-agent problem describes a situation where one party, the "principal", delegates authority to another party, called the "agent", to act on its behalf. Problems, though, arise when the agent has different objectives or interests than those of the principal. To illustrate, the agent may be more interested in personal gain than in fulfilling the principal's objectives. This can lead to an inherent conflict of interest and undermine the trust between both parties.
The principal-agent problem is often found in business settings, where shareholders or owners hire managers to run their company on their behalf. The agents, in this case, have a fiduciary duty (act in a way that will benefit someone else) to behave in the best interests of the principals, but they may also simultaneously pursue other agendas including those for

personal gain. In addition, it is the job of the principals to hold their agents accountable for their actions and manage relationships to ensure that their interests are aligned, or in other words, that the managers act as agents and not as principals themselves.

The principal-agent problem can also be seen in politics. Voters delegate authority to elected officials with whom they may have little direct contact or personal. Some voters may give preference to issues relating to social welfare or religious beliefs, while others place greater weight on issues like economic growth, crime reduction, and education reforms. Elected officials face an incentive to solve such problems based on public opinion so as to remain popular with constituents even though the solution might not align with the actual preferences of the people they officially represent. In this way, the agent's interests are different from those of the principal.

As a radically different approach to combatting the principal-agent problem, DAOs propose a democratic system of governance that lets everyone have a say in how the organization runs, which until now, has not been practical on such a large scale.

At its core, a DAO is an organization that exists solely on the Internet and is fully owned by everyone who purchases or earns its tokens, which represent equity ownership. As a key underlying principle of a decentralized autonomous organization, no single person or group of people manages the entity. Instead, its code operates on the blockchain, making it autonomous and decentralized.

In this way, a decentralized autonomous organization has no CEO, CFO, HR manager(s), or any other additional layers of upper management. All important decisions, such as how much money it will invest in which projects and for what period of time, are voted on by the DAO's participants This type of democratic decision-making can be done on a global scale by utilizing online communication tools and on-chain or off-chain voting systems.

The outcomes are then encoded in smart contracts, which are computer protocols that facilitate, verify, or enforce the negotiation of a contract between two parties. These rules can be based on certain terms accepted by both sides or set in code at the time of the organization's creation. These rules allow for a flexible service offering while providing an easy way to identify violations of conduct by any party involved. This enables and equips groups to flourish as a horizontal organization while economically incentivizing shared initiatives and disincentivizing foul play.

The organization is owned by its members who contribute to the organization. This usually involves providing value in the form of labor, funds or other resources while receiving value in return, in the form of profits (generated through the DAO's services or investments) and voting rights (as part of the organization's governance structure).

With voting rights diffused across the organization's membership, decisions are made through a distributed voting mechanism, which removes points of failure from centralized solutions while also promoting open innovation and democracy. A vote of a defined majority guarantees a successful proposal, with anyone in the DAO effectively able to make a proposal. This way, individuals, on the whole, can enjoy increased say over their present and future compared to centralized power hierarchies found in traditional companies.

As an example, decentralized reputation systems allow members to share information about service providers without worrying about manipulation from one or two power-hungry individuals. Moreover, it is easier for members to find the best service providers without needing to trust a designated authority figure. To choose which platform provider the DAO should use to mint its next NFT, members can shortlist options and propose a vote. While some individuals may have a vested interest in choosing a particular platform provider (because they own equity in that platform), their greed is effectively neutralized by the votes of others and the wisdom of the crowd.

A ranking system that takes into consideration both the past performance and reputation of a given provider may also be used to minimize transaction costs involved with finding a provider for future projects. This is regarded as an important improvement as it allows members to quickly screen different proposals based on merit instead of focusing exclusively on those who have a large number of backers.

In sum, DAOs drastically alter the way companies operate by eliminating the middle layer agents that only serve to raise operating costs while providing little value to customers. They also enable people to trust organizations and create a variety of new opportunities for members.

New Ownership Models

DAOs open the door to new forms of ownership models. One of the most interesting opportunities is when ownership is not transferred but shared.

This is the idea behind LinksDAO, which has the goal of raising funds to buy a golf course in America and democratize the country club membership experience. Rather than being owned by a wealthy individual or a closed consortium, the property will be collectively owned by all members of LinksDAO, who have equal access to the venue and voting rights over decisions about how to run the property.

Another type of group ownership model is fractionalized, e.g. when someone purchases 1% instead of 100% of an asset (i.e. real estate, music, art). Rather than antagonizing one other for possession of power, fractionalized ownership implies that multiple parties can share the same interest in a particular asset or project. Physical art, for example, is difficult to share between multiple parties, but digital art can be effectively distributed to multiple parties without having to decide who holds custody over the item.

This model of collective ownership could be a major unlock for the music industry, where musicians have traditionally been underpaid or co-opted into one-sided deals with record labels to sell their music. DAOs have the potential to break the status quo by enabling artists to fractionalize ownership of their music to a group of fans. Organized under a DAO, each member owns a fraction of the album or song's revenue rights and is therein eligible to receive royalties when the music is played on streaming sites. The DAO format also provides the artist with access to a digital community that is directly incentivized to support, promote, and market the artist's music.

Speed

In contrast to traditional corporations, which require articles of incorporation, legal expertise, bank account registration, and government approval, DAOs can be spun up in a matter of hours.

Collective incentives (skin in the game) and voting systems with automatic execution also mean that ideas that are best for the DAO can be quickly implemented and improved upon over time, whereas ideas that don't work will be revised or removed altogether.

Transparency

With no central authority or trusted third party involved, DAOs are transparent and can't be easily manipulated or influenced by outside parties because of their decentralized makeup. With the system built on blockchain technology, it becomes difficult for any outsider to manipulate data as everything is encrypted and protected by cryptography.

With everything recorded on a public blockchain ledger, it's also harder to hide insider trading from public radars. This helps to reduce (but not entirely remove) unprofessional behavior in financial markets, such as pump and dump schemes and front running. Market manipulations are also more difficult to implement since price manipulation schemes have to be voted on, which could trigger certain members to flag the plan to regulators or other interested parties.

Additionally, all corporate governance rules and internal decisions must go through a transparent consensus-based voting process where each member has input over the decision. This simple fact makes DAOs immune to the influence of centralized political bodies that are often subject to corruption, payoffs, kickbacks, tacit agreements between competitors, and hidden agendas among board members. These vulnerabilities undermine trust in many organizations, making people lose confidence and potentially causing mass protests.

While there are clear benefits to a transparent accounting and governance system, there are some drawbacks that need to be considered. Strategic decisions such as an auction bidding strategy and maximum bid limit, for instance, can be easily exploited by rival bidders at a high-stake auction.

No Middle Layer

DAOs run on a peer-to-peer network which means that most of the DAO's processes are self-executed, self-governed and not controlled by any type of central authority, gatekeeper, or middle layers of management.

The absence of a middle layer allows direct interaction between all members in a permissionless system with fewer bottlenecks, which makes it easier to share suggestions and scale compared to traditional organizations.

Under a flat, bottom-up, and opt-in structure, anyone can define, express, and lobby their ideas for the DAO. Valuable ideas are vouched by the community and if a proposal is accepted and implemented then everyone in the DAO can enjoy the upside of the initial proposal, i.e. a new software upgrade, product, or investment strategy. This means that leadership will naturally emerge from those that identify gaps and propose solutions that address and solve important problems without the need for fixed gatekeepers.

Lower Costs

DAOs typically have lower running costs when compared to traditional and centralized organizations. For one, there are no professional managers or intermediaries that would otherwise raise the cost of doing business as decisions take place via smart contracts. There are also fewer underlying costs than legacy organizations (that rely on in-person meetings and leasing physical space) as nearly all operations take place online.

Efficiency

A decentralized autonomous organization runs on self-executing codes with pre-coded rules, thus enabling it to run itself autonomously eliminating risks often associated with trust at all levels of an organization. It also enables members to achieve their given roles in an easy way by automatically executing encoded procedures. This makes DAOs highly flexible, scalable, and adaptive as they can be updated without any downtime.

Limitations

While it has been stated that DAOs provide a number of opportunities and benefits over traditional systems, there are obvious limitations and pitfalls too, as we'll explore next.

Chaotic Work Environment

The global, fast, and asynchronous nature of DAOs, with no official work hours and holidays, means that DAOs are constantly active. With no restraints, this can lead to chaos and a flurry of unproductive activity. At the contributor level, the constant messaging on communication platforms like Discord and Telegram can also cause anxiety and especially for contributors living in different time zones.

Volatility

Second, as with most projects in the crypto space, the direction of the DAO can be highly volatile without a fixed and central chain of command. Bottom-up voting may lead to a split, creating a new branch with a completely different set of rules and rendering certain tokens obsolete, for example. Alternatively, it's possible for the entire DAO to pivot based on what the community decides. This means the DAO may not stay aligned to the original vision of the DAO's founders. In this way, a social DAO may morph into a political DAO or even spiral into more nefarious behavior, also known as a dark DAO.

One of the biggest threats to a DAO, however, is a rapid decline in participation, where a failure to reach minimum vote participation or quorum can derail progress and momentum. As contributors can enter and leave at any time, this can adversely impact long-term decision-making. Also, while vesting or locking DAO tokens to ensure long-term participation might help to extend the commitment period of members, these tactics mirror the negative aspects of traditional work where employees wait out their "work sentence" with less and less enthusiasm over time.

Security

At a security level, DAOs are highly susceptible to their developers—who may be anonymous actors—failing to maintain security or even stealing funds with little chance of legal recourse. This is not to mention the inherent security flaws that come with newly and hastily formed organizations managing millions of dollars in assets. This has been an ever-present challenge since the first DAO was hacked in 2016. Five years on, $120 million in cryptocurrency was stolen from multiple cryptocurrency wallets connected to BadgerDAO in 2021.

Upfront Cost

Lastly, while operating a DAO will typically have fewer fixed costs, be wary that there can be a sizable upfront cost to establishing a DAO in the form of creating a native token and gas fees for distributing that token on the Ethereum blockchain. The high transaction cost of members to buy and sell governance tokens on the Ethereum network can also be an inhibitor to participation and a point of tension.

We saw this occur in 2021 after ConstitutionDAO failed its founding mission to buy an original copy of the United States Constitution at auction and was unable to efficiently refund contributors' donations. For some contributors, the transaction cost of refunding their donation on the Ethereum network matched or exceeded the amount of their initial donation. Ultimately, in exchange for their donations, contributors were able to redeem a governance token called $PEOPLE issued through Juicebox, which has been fluctuating wildly in price ever since.

The same problem with transaction fees can also have a negative effect with on-chain voting, where only members with a large enough incentive or high net worth are able and compelled to vote.

Despite the current situation, transaction fees for sending funds and tokens or conducting voting on the blockchain will likely come down over time as improvements are made to Ethereum[1] and other more cost-effective blockchains or layer 2 solutions are adopted.

Fiat Offramps

---

[1] Scaling developments may include modular blockchain design, zk-rollups, and sharding.

For casual obersvers, it's often overlooked that DAOs need to pay for goods and services in fiat currency. This includes paying for software subscriptions, transportation, conference tickets, food, and venue hosting that cannot be purchased using cryptocurrencies such as Bitcoin. Instead, these expenses need to be paid in local fiat currency, such as US dollars.

At present, it's common for DAO's to reimburse fiat expenses with stablecoins to a designated member who pays using their private debit card. Alternatively, DAOs that register under Wyoming's new DAO law (discussed in Chapter 6) can register an organizational bank account. Setting up a bank account, though, requires passing KYC (know your customer) for each individual with designated access to the funds and this can conflict with the decentralized and pseudonymous mindset of hardcore DAO members.

In sum, while there are ways to overcome this problem, the DAO space lacks an elegant solution for providing an open, decentralized, and shared record of fiat funds. A potential product could allow DAOs to send stablecoins pegged to a fiat currency (such as USDC) from its treasury to a third-party service provider. The stablecoins would be instantly converted to fiat via an exchange and sent via wire or ACH (automated clearing house) to a shared fiat pool with set controls over who has access to the funds. The DAO could subsequently use the pool's debit card to pay for expenses without the need for reimbursements. However, any fiat service would still require KYC verification to comply with regulations.

Unavoidable Centralization

It's important to acknowledge, too, that while DAOs are distributed groups consisting of geographically dispersed individuals, it's impossible for everything to be fully decentralized. Depending on the DAO, there are typically instances of centralization embedded into the organization as well as a legitimate need for that control of power. Examples include exclusive power and access for designated experts to work on important code and security projects—preventing unwanted harm caused by new entrants or malicious forces. The DAO's original governance rules, which are written into smart contracts or blockchain protocol, are also an example of upfront centralization.[2]

On top of this, since DAOs rely on consensus-based decision-making, it's possible for a block of contributors in one region, such as North America or Europe, to control the dialogue, power, and votes over the long run. Likewise, it's common for small groups of people to hold the majority of the available governance tokens and thereby control the outcome of governance decisions.

In later chapters, we will explore how individuals and organizations can benefit from decentralized technology and study best practices for designing and tooling decentralized autonomous organizations.

---

[2] Shermin Voshmgir, "Token Economy: How the Web3 reinvents the Internet", *Token Kitchen*, Second Edition, 2020, p134.

2

FROM CENTRALIZED TO DECENTRALIZED

To understand the advantages and limitations of DAOs, it's important to understand the fundamentals of its opposite, a centralized or centrally controlled organization.

By design, a centralized organization has one or multiple owners who enjoy the power to make decisions on behalf of the entire organization. They do so by hiring managers and employees who work for and under them, effectively forming a pyramid of individuals that make up a hierarchical organizational structure. This structure can create resentment when projects are poorly run or promises are broken as upper management is not accountable to anyone below them in the pyramid.

The vast majority of corporations we know today are centralized and operate under this described model. Still, it's also possible for this model to be a runaway success, but this relies heavily on trust. A corporation can't control everything itself. It has to trust its employees and managers to enforce trust by whatever means possible. Trust in turn parents responsibility; employees feel responsible for doing their job because if they don't, they or others might lose their jobs or be demoted as a means of punishment.

Managers, however, are prone to exploit their position of privilege, which can undermine trust and their underlings' loyalty to the organization. Consider the two following examples of a breakdown in trust.

1) An employee steals money or products from the company's inventory.

2) A manager uses their position of power to pass on negative consequences to someone who works under them.

Both instances undermine an organization's ability to control its internal affairs. Hence, in order to enforce trust, centralized organizations rely on constructing social rules and narratives. As an example, employees are expected to dress in professional attire when they attend meetings or presentations outside the office in a deliberate attempt to appear trustworthy. Employees may also be discouraged from discussing specific topics at certain times and keeping their conversations at work to PG-13.

This display of social engineering looms as one of the biggest problems in centralized organizations today. Whether they're aware of it or not, people are naturally susceptible to the influence of those around them. Managers might try and enforce stricter rules by convincing everyone else that it's a strictly enforced rule—even if it is not. This brand of manipulation is difficult to catch because most people aren't sufficiently aware of themselves and others to know what is actually true or not.

These problems coalesce and culminate in a large network of internal stress inside centralized organizations. Employees feel stressed because they have an elevated point of responsibility but can only get away with very little. Managers, meanwhile, feel stressed because they need to keep the company profitable and manage others while making sure no one notices their own flaws and failures to abide by company etiquette. Stress, it should be emphasized, leads to a variety of issues that impacts everything from employees' health to high-profile lawsuits made against the organization.

The second constraint of centralized power is that information flows top-down, which means that only authorized persons can access certain information while others are directly excluded. Senior management, for example, knows how much revenue the company is generating at any given time while regular employees are privy only to information about their daily tasks without a broad snapshot view of how profitable the company is and its long-term prospects.

This reinforces a hierarchical organizational structure based on unequal access to information. The more power and resources you have in the company, the higher your rank and the more information you receive. By denying lower-level employees power and resources to enact change or pursue new goals, traditional hierarchical structures stifle innovation.

Combined with the economic inefficiency of increasing layers of rigid bureaucracy inside the organization as the entity matures, this ultimately contributes to the long-term decline of the organization. According to Innosight's biennial corporate longevity report, the 30-35 year average tenure of S&P 500 companies in the late 1970s is forecast to shrink to 15-20 years during this decade.[3] This statistic suggests that the internal structure of centralized corporations is inherently flawed and susceptible to the fast pace of technological innovation and global competition.

Stagnant innovation and bloated bureaucracy, it should be said, can exist too within decentralized organizations. However, it is significantly limited by the integration of blockchain technology. With all the rules codified under fixed principles—indicating how to deal with various problems—the flow of decisions can be accelerated to keep up with the fast pace of technological development. This opens up space for talented people to focus on innovative initiatives, eliminate problems like middle management inefficiencies, and therein disrupt the traditional labor theory of property.

Popularized by the English philosopher and physician John Locke (1632-1704), labor theory of property argues that labor can be exploited by means of private property norms. To explain why, it is necessary to define the following terms. First, "means of production" refers to the physical resources an organization owns; this includes offices, factories, and raw materials. Second, "labor" refers to people working for an organization. Private property norms prohibit workers from leaving their jobs without compensation. If labor cannot leave freely, then it is being exploited because employers are receiving more value than they are giving back in the form of wages.

Third, "property rights", or rules about who owns what, enable managers to extract value from employees using techniques such as target setting and firing anyone who does not meet their targets. If property rights grant managers power over laborers by default rather than grant laborers power over themselves through democratic processes, then laborers are inevitably being exploited.

---

[3] S. Patrick Viguerie, Ned Calder & Brian Hindo, "2021 Corporate Longevity Forecast", *Innosight*, May 2021, www.innosight.com/insight/creative-destruction.

DAOs, though, shift "means of production" and "labor" from separate entities to essentially everyone. If the entity owns nothing and nobody works for it, then a decentralized autonomous organization cannot exploit "labor". Instead of one person or group being in charge of tasks, multiple and perhaps unlimited individuals contribute to the completion of tasks. In some scenarios, the more people contributing, the better the overall outcome.[4]

However, unlike how most centralized corporations exist and function today, there are no specific power roles within a DAO. In general, everyone exists on the same playing field. Moreover, every member has an equal say when making decisions about what direction the company should take. In a traditional company like Amazon, Jeff Bezos and upper management retain controlling authority over whether Amazon will accept cryptocurrency as a settlement layer on their platforms. Under a DAO structure, though, such a decision could be voted upon by all participants and not gatekeepers at certain levels of the organization. This represents an important shift from top-down decision-making to collective decision-making.

DAOs, therein, exist as horizontal organizations with few to no command-and-control structures. Members are free to issue proposals and vote at any time. Also, because decisions are executed on the chain, a successful vote automatically releases funds to the proposed project or initiative without central interference. Under this model, the ideas and actions of DAO members are directly diffused into the organization's operations.

Moreover, each individual can be rewarded proportionately according to the amount of work they contributed. In a traditional corporation, employees are paid a salary irrespective of their performance. In a DAO, the amount of money or financial reward (i.e. equity/tokens) is usually directly proportional to how much work someone has provided. In other words, each individual is paid for what they have

---

[4] Traditionally, in order for a DAO to be successful, there needs to be a reasonably large and active community of participants. The DAO that was hacked in 2016 had over $150 million worth of Ether at the time of the hack. However, the DAO was unable to attract new participants and eventually failed due to a lack of funding.

contributed. At the same time, there's no sitting around expecting a fixed reward at regular intervals of time.

However, how do you know people will follow through with what they say they will do? How can you check they completed what they reported? And how can you trust others especially people you've never met?

The Case for Smart Contracts

The key characteristic of a DAO is that no person, group, or computer can force any other member to do anything against their will. Members must instead convince one another through debate and consensus, which means that all members have equal say over how the DAO functions.

A major problem with implementing this type of organization on traditional servers is there can be no central server process that keeps track of all interactions between people as then the central server would essentially be making decisions for all members of the group.

DAOs, though, trade the traditional operating system of an organization with a crypto-native software stack based on a peer-to-peer network. As a result, DAOs communicate and coordinate through a network where anyone within the network has access to all information stored on every computer. The computers connected to the network don't need to know who each node is, and instead, they only need to know how to transmit messages between one another. This way, no person or entity can gain control over all interactions in the network.

To reach consensus, DAOs rely on what are called smart contracts, which is code deployed on decentralized servers that run without the aid of humans. This enables the DAO to operate autonomously and transparently.

Smart contracts are used for processes like multi-sig banking; when you want another party (e.g. a lawyer) to approve a transaction (e.g. sending money between your accounts) but you don't want them to control the wallet once it is sent—or for more complicated technology like Ethereum, which lets users store and send value in the form of tokens.

Using smart contracts, people who don't know each other can make deals with one another without an expensive back-and-forth process where both parties risk getting cheated. Instead of needing a manager to ensure employees and contractors are faithful to their responsibilities, smart contracts automate supervision and codify trust. Given that everyone's contribution is tracked by a transparent ledger, there are far fewer chances of anyone trying to cheat the system.

Another big innovation is that smart contracts enable people from all around the world to interact freely with each participant's identity and reputation cryptographically hashed into the blockchain. This allows participants to retain anonymity while still enjoying strong security and trust within the DAO thanks to its transparent nature. Olympus DAO, whose market capitalization exploded to USD $4 billion in 2021, was created by an incognito developer who calls himself "Zeus", for example.

A Return to Decentralization

The common thought in DAO literature purports a narrative that because decentralized organizations are a counterargument to centralized ones, they are therefore radically new and different. This chain of thought supports the view that the decentralized organization of groups is unconventional and relatively untested.

However, if we scroll the time roll of human history to the left, we see that humans weren't always organized in a hierarchical structure under an obvious center of command. For thousands of years, hunter-gather societies operated under a mostly flat and egalitarian structure that organized humans into small tribes or bands.[5] With few resources to distribute, there was no full-time leaders, bureaucrats, or hereditary chiefs. Influence, too, was more evenly balanced between the sexes. Naturally, some members were more vocal, persuasive, and influential than others, but they could also become a target and risk exile if they overexerted their position over others. In general, decisions were thus reached by group consensus and, for the large part, carried out peacefully.

Consider, for example, hunter-gather societies in Polynesia that held council meetings and maintained a tradition of

---

[5] Jared Diamond, "Guns, Germs, and Steel: The Fates of Human Society", *W. W. Norton & Company*, First Edition, 1999.

resolving disputes peacefully. Jared Diamond, in his book *Guns, Germs, and Steel: The Fates of Human Society*, highlights the example of the Moriori people on New Zealand's Chatham Islands—who up until an outside invasion—regularly held council meetings that promoted "peace, friendship, and division of resources".[6]

In fact, based on the research of nomadic tribes compiled for the journal *Science* in 2013, anthropologists Douglas Fry and Patrik Soderberg made the conclusion that hunter-gathers are more inclined to talk out their grievances than to resort to violence. Their study suggests that most murders in hunter-gather societies originate from interpersonal feuds and jealousy rather than conflict at the group level.[7]

In the past—prior to "civilization" and private property norms—members of nomad groups were free to vote with their feet. If their opinions no longer aligned with the tribe, they could quickly pack up their belongings, move onto the next valley and find a new tribe. As Rutger Brenman observes in *Humankind: A Hopeful History*, it was remarkably common to switch tribes or even swap members.[8]

The later establishment of sedentary and farming-based societies gradually supplanted the open, peaceful, and flat structure of tribes throughout much of the globe. A combination of factors, including population acceleration, large-scale resource distribution, full-time standing armies, and religious doctrine pressed humans into highly centralized and male-dominated social structures. No longer was it practical to call a council meeting or trust your neighbor.

With the stakes exponentially higher, self-interest ran riot. Natural and charismatic leaders devised new myths and propaganda—including rule by divine right or imagined racism—to unite their subjects, control resources, and

---

[6] Jared Diamond, "Guns, Germs, and Steel: The Fates of Human Society", *W. W. Norton & Company*, First Edition, 1999.
[7] Fry and Soderberg compiled a database of every reliable and well-documented incident of lethal aggression spanning the last two centuries across 21 nomadic forager societies. Of the 148 incidents they compiled, over half involved one killer and one victim, 22% involved multiple killers and multiple victims, and one-third constituted an inter-group conflict. Most murders were motivated by sexual jealousy, revenge (based on a previous murder), insults, or an interpersonal quarrel.
[8] Rutger Brenman, "Humankind: A Hopeful History", *Little, Brown and Company*, 2020.

maintain cooperation. This replaced peer-to-peer trust between small groups of individuals and bundled it into a centralized organization called a chiefdom, a church, state, empire, or country, who made decisions on behalf of their trusting or coerced subjects. This pattern of control—locked up in human-engineered narrative—has dominated ever since, as documented in Yuval Noah Harari's best-selling book *Sapiens: A Brief History of Humankind.*

Consider the example of modern corporations and how trust is bundled there. Over the long-term, industrialists realized that it's easier to collaborate with a group of people by formally hiring them and signing contracts under the guise of a fictional entity—called a corporation—than it is to enter a personal agreement where they collect a majority of the profits and someone else does majority of the work. Likewise, it is easier to generate passionate patriotism and pride towards a fictional entity, such as a country, than to one person. As Nassim Nicholas Taleb writes in *The Bed Of Procrustes: Philosophical And Practical Aphorisms,* "We find it to be in extremely bad taste for individuals to boast of their accomplishments; but when countries do so we call it 'national pride.'"[9]

It is only now, with the advent of blockchain technology, that trust can be unbundled and reverted to a peer-to-peer system of validation, based on code instead of narrative, legal contracts, corporate documents, or empty promises.

Decentralized autonomous organizations are not perfect, as we will explore in coming chapters, but there is an alternative—that's not as novel and untested as many people are led to believe.

---

[9] Nassim Nicholas Taleb, "The Bed Of Procrustes: Philosophical And Practical Aphorisms", *Random House,* 2010.

3

THE EARLY GENESIS OF DAOS

Decentralized organizations have been a topic of discussion since the early days of the cryptocurrency evolution. In 2013, Vitalik Buterin, the founder of the Ethereum blockchain, registered a Swiss company called Ethereum Switzerland GmbH (EthSuisse). He subsequently wrote about its legal status as a decentralized autonomous organization before later closing that entity a year later.

The original basis of decentralization was inspired by Adam Back in 1997 as part of a proof-of-work algorithm called Hashcash. The algorithm was subsequently integrated into anti-spam systems and later adopted by Bitcoin as a mining function. In 1998, Nick Szabo, a computer scientist and cryptographer, realized that the algorithm could also be applied to other use cases beyond anti-spam systems. He proposed several different applications for a decentralized financial system including one based on autonomous agents. Under this system, called "bit gold", every transaction would be enforced with tamperproof remote attestation (the way most electronic contracts work today). Attestation refers to a declaration that something exists or is the case.

Szabo's other influential breakthrough came with his work on smart contracts. Programmed to complete specific tasks on an ongoing basis, smart contracts provide the key underlying infrastructure for running a DAO on the blockchain.

Szabo's ideas on decentralization and smart contracts reached many researchers including Hal Finney, Wei Dai, and finally, Satoshi Nakamoto. It was Nakamoto who realized that these same concepts could be applied to not just business contracts but also digital currencies and entire voting systems.

Around the time of 2009, several different protocols were either proposed or created independently in attempts to achieve a decentralized system of exchange. These systems included Nick Szabo's bit gold (which was built but never published), Wei Dai's b-money, Hal Finney's RPOW (Reusable Proofs of Work), Adam Back's Hashcash (still in use today within Bitcoin), and finally, Satoshi Nakamoto's Bitcoin.

The concept of a DAO, meanwhile, was introduced by computer programmer and activist Daniel Larimer in his 2013 blog article titled *The Hidden Costs of Bitcoin*.[10] In this post, Larimer outlines several different applications for a decentralized financial system. Of note, Larimer uses the term "Decentralized Autonomous Corporation" (DAC) to describe an entity with source code representing its bylaws and token holders as its shareholders. The DAC's purpose, according to Larimer, is to maximize value for its token holders by performing activities on the free market and paying for services using its own shares, referred to as *tokens*.

In a separate blog post, this time published by Daniel's father, Stan Larimer, questions are put forward over whether Bitcoin would be better applied as a DAC rather than as a currency.[11] Stan Larimer also further defines a DAC as an entity run by an incorruptible set of business rules that can be executed independently without human involvement. This premise was based on the idea of open-source software distributed across a network of computers (also known as "nodes") that could be publicly audited.

Following the writing of these two blog posts, Vitalik Buterin published a series of three blog posts outlining and analyzing the technical challenges of developing a fully distributed corporation on the Bitcoin blockchain.

However, it was the Ethereum White Paper, again published by Buterin in later 2013, which helped to popularize the term "decentralized autonomous organization".[12] In explaining the definition of a decentralized autonomous organization, Buterin wrote the following:

"The general concept of a 'decentralized autonomous organization' is that of a virtual entity that has a certain set of members or shareholders which, perhaps with a 67% majority, have the right to spend the entity's funds and modify its code.

---

[10] Daniel Larimer, "The Hidden Costs of Bitcoin", *Letstalkbitcoin.com*, September 7, 2013.
[11] Stan Larimer, "Bitcoin and the Three Laws of Robotics", *Letstalkbitcoin.com*, September 14, 2013.
[12] Vitalik Buterin, "Ethereum Whitepaper", *Ethereum.org*, December 2013.

The members would collectively decide on how the organization should allocate its funds. Methods for allocating a DAO's funds could range from bounties, salaries to even more exotic mechanisms such as an internal currency to reward work. This essentially replicates the legal trappings of a traditional company or nonprofit but using only cryptographic blockchain technology for enforcement."

In the same white paper, Buterin addresses the difference between Larimer's "decentralized autonomous corporation" and a "decentralized autonomous organization", writing:

"So far much of the talk around DAOs has been around the 'capitalist' model of a 'decentralized autonomous corporation' (DAC) with dividend-receiving shareholders and tradable shares; an alternative, perhaps described as a 'decentralized autonomous community', would have all members have an equal share in the decision making and require 67% of existing members to agree to add or remove a member."

In summary, Buterin differentiated a DAC from a DAO based on scope, explaining that the former is a type of DAO catering to for-profit entities, whereas the latter also extends to non-profit entities, while still acknowledging that such entities could derive income. It's said that Daniel Larimer later agreed to drop the term "corporation" in favor of "organization" to minimize potential legal scrutiny.[13]

The DAO

The first DAO was created in early 2016 by the now-defunct blockchain company Slock.it. As a decentralized autonomous organization running on the recent Ethereum blockchain ledger, the goal of The DAO was to provide an autonomous vehicle for fund management without the need for traditional fund managers. Specifically, The DAO allowed individual contributors to pitch their ideas to the community, receive funding, invest in projects, and vote on investment proposals in proportion to their financial contribution to the organization. By issuing tokens for contributions made in Ether (ETH), The DAO raised over USD $150 million through an initial

---

[13] Sven Riva, "Decentralized Autonomous Organizations (DAOs) as Subjects of Law – the Recognition of DAOs in the Swiss Legal Order", *University of Neuchâtel*, 2020.

crowdfunding campaign. This made it the largest crowdfunded project in history at the time.

However, only weeks after its launch, a hacker exploited a vulnerability in The DAO's code and siphoned 3.6 million Ether (worth approximately $50 million at the time). This led to a controversial split in the Ethereum community and a fork of the network. The fork resulted in the dual existence today of Ethereum and Ethereum Classic (the original ledger that was not altered in response to the devastating hack).

The DAO, meanwhile, was ultimately shut down in 2017 following another hacking incident that resulted in the theft of $170 million worth of Ether.

While The DAO was ultimately unsuccessful, it served as a valuable lesson in collective governance for the Ethereum community and helped to spur the development of new security measures and governance protocols. It also demonstrated the potential of blockchain technology to support decentralized organizations operating without traditional forms of governance or oversight. In light of these successes and failures, The DAO is often cited as one of the most important projects in the history of blockchain technology. It also helped set the stage for a wave of new DAOs that followed.

The Summer of DeFi

Fearing a repeat and more lost funds, the next wave of DAOs were more vigilant when it came to programming and security standards, and while it took time to reassure individual investors, it was incentive design that ultimately revived the DAO movement.

Using overt financial incentives to encourage participation and investment, the next generation of DAOs emerged. These DAOs attracted capital using yield farming (rewarding members with tokens for performing actions like lending, borrowing, staking, or providing other forms of asset liquidity) as an incentive, which led to an explosion of activity in the summer of 2020 spearheaded by the likes of Yearn Finance (YFI) and Uniswap.

Operating under the banner of DeFi (decentralized finance), these DAOs released governance tokens to incentivize open and community-led projects as well as rewarding contributors with equity in the DAO—not just rewarding the original VC investors and the development team.

The summer of DeFi subsequently opened the door to attracting attention from developers, investors, and entrepreneurs. This led to the development of more sophisticated open-finance systems and new software tools to manage decentralized organizations.

In June 2020, an on-chain lending protocol named Compound decentralized itself by transferring operations and ownership of the protocol to the community. Importantly, this gave community members control of margin requirements, interest rates, as well as the protocol's fee-generating reserve assets collected from borrowers (the organization's primary cash flow).

Compound devised a novel model to distribute governance in the form of native tokens called COMP. Compound dropped these tokens to users who provided liquidity and borrowed from the protocol. In this way, every user of Compound instantly became a stakeholder, which in turn, converted a percentage of token holders into active contributors and voters. These members had an overt reason to act in the best interests of the DAO, as their time and energy designing and voting on governance proposals would be rewarded via their equity stake.

Other types of DAOs emerged too, especially on the back of NFT (non-fungible token) adoption. This included collector DAOs like PleasrDAO and Flamingo who allow token holders to vote on what art to purchase, which artists to endorse, what to do with the art piece (i.e. fractionize and tokenize the art), as well as other collective decisions including treasury management and marketing. As with DeFi projects, the outcomes of these votes are directly executed on the blockchain.

Collector and other DAO types also built upon the precedent set by Compound and the DeFi sector to bond governance with direct financial incentives. For members, this ensures that the long-term growth and success of the organization benefit them personally.

Today there are many fully-deployed DAOs active in a variety of sectors including fundraising, media, real estate lending, art collection, and climate activism. Started on the Internet by a small group of like-minded individuals, these organizations are now managing billions of dollars in assets without the need for intermediaries or a CEO.

4

HOW DO DAOS WORK?

Despite their name, DAOs are not entirely autonomous; you still need humans to design and create decision frameworks (coded into smart contracts) to ensure the DAO is defined in advance and governed effectively.

To define and design a DAO, there are three core components: the token, the treasury, and the governance protocol. The token is what gives participants in the DAO the right to participate and directly invest in the organization. The treasury is the organization's equivalent to a bank account and asset holdings. The governance protocol ensures that all participants in the DAO have a fair say in decision-making and the future direction of the organization.

Tokens

In traditional corporations, ownership is represented by share certificates held by shareholders, with voting rights for shareholders determined by the number of shares they own. The more shares somebody owns, the more votes they have to cast at shareholder meetings. In contrast, ownership and voting rights in a DAO are reflected using tokens that represent how many votes each participant has based on the organization's governance protocol. Usually, the more tokens one holds, the more weight their vote will carry on governance decisions. A minimum number of tokens might also be required to join the DAO, though this threshold is normally relatively low for new DAOs.

Tokens can be traded freely on exchanges similar to other cryptocurrencies including Bitcoin and Ether, which means these tokens can accumulate or lose value on the open market. As more people join the network or invest in the DAO's token, the value of the token will appreciate based on higher demand. Conversely, the value of the token can depreciate over time if there is an exodus of members and token holders, which is generally an indicator of negative sentiment towards a particular DAO.

If someone wants to become a member of a given DAO, they simply need to prove ownership of the DAOs' native token, and in some cases, receive a nomination from an existing member or join through some other means of criteria. Still, in most cases, participation is permissionless—especially in the case of newly formed DAOs. This means that anyone holding a set amount of the native token is automatically eligible to participate.

The purchase-to-participate approach via a native token helps to self-select members with a proactive interest in the DAO's founding mission and activities. Some DAOs, however, are private and their tokens are not available for sale on the open market. To join, prospective members typically submit a proposal to join based on their skills and experience or are directly invited by the DAO. New members are subsequently allocated a share of tokens or asked to provide a specific service in exchange for governance tokens.

Tokens can also be earned and received as part of a reward for member contributions. Members of Friends With Benefits, a social network of thinkers and creators in a private Discord server, can earn tokens by being active in Discord, attending community calls, hosting recurring events, and overseeing collaborative programs. Members of the media DAO Forefront, meanwhile, can earn tokens by writing a content post, editing another contributor's post, or distributing posts online.

Treasury

A DAO's treasury underwrites the organization's ability to finance and deploy capital to achieve its mission. DAOs are initially seeded with a first round of capital, in the form of governance tokens minted by the DAO and sold to members.

To demonstrate, if a DAO mints 10,000 governance tokens and sells 5,000 of them to its founding members for 1 ETH, then the DAO's treasury will consist of 5,000 governance tokens and 5,000 ETH. As the DAO grows, the remaining tokens can be sold or new tokens may be minted according to the rules coded in the DAO's smart contracts.

Minting and selling unique NFTs is another common method to generate revenue for the DAO's treasury. Some DAOs, including BanklessDAO, even sell their own merchandise to raise funds.

The assets held by the DAO's treasury can then be used for funding projects, web development, audits, insurance, grants, day-to-day costs, emergency outlays, and even a potential merger and acquisition.

Lastly, treasuries not only need best management practices to function but also innovation and strategy in order to improve the DAO's long-term market position and to build a portfolio of investments that are aligned with its overarching goals. Common strategies for managing a DAO's treasury will be discussed later in Chapter 6.

Governance

As DAOs grow in size, how to govern the community and distribute resources takes on added importance. Governance answers the need to involve members in voting and decision-making in order to effectively distribute resources, manage projects, and carry out the mission of the DAO.

While governance can soak up significant effort to coordinate and execute, this effort can be radically reduced using smart contracts linked to the treasury (multi-sig wallet) and online voting applications like Snapshot. Replacing manual governance procedures such as board meetings, annual general meetings, postal votes, and other legacy processes with governance software is one of the key advantages of running an organization as a DAO. Trusted technology, in the form of the blockchain and smart contracts, makes it easy to align resources with incentives and interests. Governance no longer needs to rely on one leader or be subject to a single point of failure, as most operations can run entirely on code.

The governance rules for a DAO can be as unique and decentralized as its members wish it to be. A DAO can have one core leadership team or a council that makes all the proposals and then allows the community to vote (more analogous to a board of a company). Conversely, a DAO can operate as a fully transparent and decentralized organization where anyone can issues proposals and vote on decisions to direct and grow the organization.

Aside from full and open community governance, there is the additional option of delegated governance where specific individuals or committees (such as working groups) vote on behalf of other members. While this reintroduces a degree of centralization, delegated governance helps to avoid dragged-out and multi-week voting processes and is prominent when it comes to highly technical decisions such as DAO security and treasury management.

To vote, members of the DAO need to fulfill basic voting criteria regarding governance rights in the DAO, established in the founding governance document. The two primary tactics to distribute governance rights to DAO members are fungible tokens (i.e. ERC-20) and non-fungible tokens (NFT, i.e. ERC-721).

DAOs typically adopt their own governance token in the form of a fungible token, while other DAOs use NFTs, such as unique land released as an NFT in a virtual world or art NFTs. Both forms of tokens can be used to vote on a governance platform such as Snapshot, and voting may be weighted according to a member's token holdings or based on a one-person-one-vote system.

By their very nature, fungible tokens help to promote a liquid internal economy of buying and selling (as opposed to hoarding NFTs), which makes it easy to reward contributors. Conversely, with NFT-based governance, there is typically less scrutiny from authorities regarding securities law (especially in the U.S.). Of course, you will need to seek professional legal advice to assess your DAO's specific situation and the decision between fungible and non-fungible token-based governance.

Some DAOs incorporate a mixed system of fungible and non-fungible token governance. In the virtual world Decentraland, members of the DAO receive 1 vote for each unit of MANA (a fungible ERC-20 token) they own and 2,000 votes per parcel of private land (a non-fungible ERC-721 token) they own.

Another popular strategy is to deliver tokens to current or former users' wallets as part of an airdrop. This is a special tactic to spread awareness, build ownership, and retroactively reward early participants of the DAO's network. While this tactic won't apply to newly formed organizations, established

DeFi projects, for instance, can retrospectively grant tokens to past users of the protocol to shape its future governance structure. This is the path Uniswap took when it dropped its governance token called UNI to everyone who had previously used the Uniswap protocol. The airdrop helped to change and distribute the governance power of the organization by incentivizing a wide group of members to engage with decision-making through voting rights endowed by the Uniswap DAO.

Guilds

As DAOs evolve, it's common to allocate tasks across working committees, also known as guilds. The purpose of a guide is to pool talent and create a network of groups that can handle narrowly-defined tasks, such as onboarding, communications, newsletter publishing, translation, and one-off projects.

In general, guilds are highly focused on outcome-based tasks and project delivery relevant to the core running of the DAO.

Sub-DAOs

As DAOs scale and guilds take on more responsibility, some working committees evolve and branch out into their own sub-DAOs. Also referred to as sub-committees, sub-groups, or pods, these units enjoy more autonomy, responsibility, resources as well as space to innovate than a typical guild.

Moving further on-chain and sometimes using their own software tools or plugins, additional responsibilities of a sub-DAO may include internal governance, compensation, and allocation of responsibilities.

Like guilds, sub-DAOs are still relied upon for executing duties relevant to the wider DAO, but they have more autonomy over how that work is done and how contributors are compensated. In other words, they have more say over defining the rules and creating their own. In addition, the scope of their work generally branches out into broader categories such as UX (user experience), security, marketing, investment, M&A, and programming development.

By attracting relevant talent and setting KPIs, sub-DAOs can improve the DAO's efficiency as well as streamline operational cadence by reducing time and effort spent rallying the full organization to vote on niche or highly technical decisions.

At the same time, sub-DAOs help DAOs to resist the stagnancy that commonly afflicts and hamstrings traditional organizations. As an organization grows larger and more successful, it becomes harder to replicate disruptive innovation and introduce change. Rather than innovating, the organization is more focused on sustaining its present market position and optimizing its existing product line or service offering.

Sub-DAOs offer a path to bypass this trap by creating a distinct culture and ethos that encourages innovation, while at the same time accessing financial resources and talent passed on by the parent DAO. By design, the sub-DAO is able to iterate and move faster as decisions related to the new product, service, or technology are siloed from the standard practices of the past.

To function independently, sub-DAOs often use special tools (covered further in the next chapter) for managing resources and partitioning member authorization. In some cases, it's possible to use smart contracts to set up and run a sub-DAO or there's the other option of no-code tools created by DAO's like Orca Protocol without the need for development expertise. The Orca Protocol allows you to create authorized groups that can manage certain functions within a DAO, allowing different sub-DAOs to manage and operate tasks independently.

To stay accountable for their work, the sub-DAO should provide a regular recap or report on their progress, and, every few months or so, invite the parent DAO to complete an audit of their work. Specifically, the DAO needs to assess whether key performance indicators have been met and whether they should call a DAO-wide vote to veto, course correct, or change the scope, resources, and funding of the sub-DAO. If the sub-DAO is performing and posting consistent results, then the parent DAO might allocate further resources including funding and personnel, for example.

In more rare cases, the runaway success of a new product, service, investment, or technology developed by the sub-DAO might prompt a fork and a new spin-off DAO, in which the sub-DAO effectively becomes its own independent DAO. A sub-DAO with its own funds, smart contracts, and governance mechanisms can be ported with minimal friction as most resources can be sent on-chain to the new entity. The stakeholder or member base of the original DAO can also be forked or shared between the two DAOs. Flamingo (original DAO) and Neon (former sub-DAO), for example, have active members across both DAOs despite their independent status.

Alternatively, a parent DAO might decide to merge two sub-DAOs as part of a restructure that realigns interests and sets out to accomplish shared goals.

5

TYPES OF DAOS

As with centralized organizations, there are many practical use cases for DAOs, including different goals, frameworks, and tools for communities to pool resources and start a movement. In this chapter, we will review the most common types of DAOs.

Investment DAOs

In an industry dominated by speculation, there has been a surge in investment DAOs in recent times. This type of DAO bands investors to chase high returns in the crypto market while leveraging large amounts of capital and "wisdom of the crowd" investment strategies. In fact, the horizontal and collective decision-making framework of a DAO renders itself highly suitable for investment strategy. Analogous to the behavior of social insects, the hive mind structure of a DAO allows a group of diverse investors to think and act as a network of minds along with shared access to a very large pool of resources.

An example is an autonomous, decentralized, and transparent venture capital fund that holds shares of several promising ventures and invests in these ventures or projects at opportune times. The DAO's goal is to deliver returns on its investments for its members while ensuring the success of all investee companies through ongoing funding rounds. However, given that investment DAOs require an initial investment from members to achieve associated growth, as an individual member, you should not expect an immediate return on your investment, especially from newly formed DAOs.

While investment DAOs are subject to more legal restrictions than other DAOs, they still offer relatively low barriers to entry for individual investors than traditional investment clubs. Having said that, investment DAOs sometimes limit their membership numbers to avoid attention from the Securities & Exchange Commission (SEC). Under the 2,000 Investor Limit, a company that has 2,000 or more individual investors with over USD $10 million in combined assets must file its financials with the SEC. In addition, an investment club can only have up to 99 Accredited Investors; the remaining members (under the cap of 2000) must be Qualified Purchasers, which requires a higher threshold of net worth than an Accredited Investor.

Investment DAOs include MetaCartel, theLAO, Flamingo, Komerebi, UdacityFund, BitDAO, Free Company, and Duck DAO.

Social DAOs

Rather than focus on investing, social DAOs concentrate their resources and focus on developing social capital among people with similar interests. As Cooper Turnley explains, "Where social media turned everybody into a media company, Social DAOs turn every group chat into a digital business."

Examples of social DAOs include Friends with Benefits, Seed Club, Metafam, ProsperDAO, SongCamp, Proof of Humanity, TheWIPmeetup, FiatLuxDAO, and Radical.

Grants DAOs

As the decentralized version of traditional crowdfunding, grants DAOs enable online communities to donate and allocate funds for open grant proposals that are subsequently voted on by the community. Examples of grants DAOs include virtual world DAOs tied to Decentraland and The Sandbox game that help to distribute funding to artists and in-world projects based on member voting.

Another example is the UniSwap Grants program, which has a mountain of capital (over $3 billion) and funds projects proposed by members of its community. The DAO accepts funding applications for both big and small web3[14] projects in usability

---

[14] The web 1 era consisted of a one-to-one relationship between users and the webmaster with limited social functionality and the notion of a community. The web2 era delivered a many-to-one relationship between users and the website. Users, for example, could curate links and posts on platforms like Digg and Reddit, and, as a community make decisions on what content would feature on the site through an

(to improve the user experience), community (grow the ecosystem), and tooling (improving the developer experience). Funding applications can be made at unigrants.org.

Other examples of grants DAOs include MetaCartel Ventures, MolochDAO, Audius Grants, Mint Fun, Sevens Foundation, Compound Grants, and Aave Grants.

Virtual World DAOs

Some but not all virtual worlds in the evolving metaverse utilize a DAO formation to govern their respective world. The existence of a DAO provides virtual citizens with a feeling of involvement in their chosen world and a platform to invest in projects, share ideas, and manage the community.

In Decentraland, landowners automatically receive voting rights via their land tokens, which allows them to influence decisions on the future development and daily running of Decentraland. This includes voting on what kinds of wearable items are allowed, content moderation, as well as land and auction policies. This process of governance differs from how important decisions are made in Second Life or on content platforms such as YouTube and Facebook where decisions that directly affect users are made behind closed doors.

Examples include Decentraland (Decentraland DAO) and Sandbox (The Foundation).

Service DAOs

To service the growth and proliferation of DAO projects, service DAOs provide crypto-native resources, including marketing, web3 development, legal services, and design. Aragon, for instance, offers a decentralized dispute resolution protocol called Aragon Court, which is designed to help handle subjective disputes that cannot be resolved by smart contracts alone.

---

upvote and downvote system. However, the communities on these sites could never actually own the net results. They could impact the homepage and curate the links but they could not capture and enjoy the upside of their contributions. Web3 now allows for a grassroots approach to building products, brand-building at the community level, and collaboration through distributed ownership via tokens and giving equity back to individual contributors.

40

Similar to Fiverr and Upwork, there are also open marketplaces such as Timerr and Braintrust where DAOs can find crypto professionals for different lines of work. There is also Vector DAO, which offers design services, and MetaFactory which provides fashion merchandise that DAOs can sell (such as t-shirts and caps) among many other services including 'digiphysical goods' that connect multiple worlds via NFTs.

These various service platforms are DAOs themselves and are set up to offer both users and freelancers equity via the issuance of native governance tokens.

Other examples include PartyDAO, Syndicate, MetaverseDAO, YGG UniWhales, HoneyDAO, OPOLIS, Yam DAO, and Aladdin DAO.

Collector DAOs

With NFTs exploding onto the scene in 2020-2021, collector DAOs pool resources and industry knowledge to snatch up the best collectibles on the market. As PleasrDAO has demonstrated, collector DAOs can also help to publicize and promote longevity behind the work of supported artists. PleasrDAO has achieved success in a string of high-profile auctions, including the Snowden NFT purchased for $5 million, the Wu-Tang Clan album for $4 million (later minted as an NFT), and the original Dogecoin meme NFT for $225 million.

Another example of a high-profile auction carried out by a collector DAO was the attempted purchase of an original copy of the United States Constitution in November 2021. Helmed by a small core of contributors and developers, ConstitutionDAO was spun up as an attempt to purchase the historical document.

Rallying under the hashtag #wagbtc (we're all gonna buy the Constitution) on Twitter, ConstitutionDAO mobilized 17,000 people who donated a combined total of USD $46 million in ETH. This translated to a median contribution of USD $205 per member (based on Ethereum addresses). In exchange for their contribution, members received a token designed to distribute collective ownership of the purchased item.

Leading up to the auction, ConstitutionDAO was in discussion with multiple public organizations including the Smithsonian

41

and New York Public Library regarding options to present the physical memorabilia. This included free viewing for token holders, token giveaways, and accompanying educational material about web3 to supplement a potential exhibition.

ConstitutionDAO ultimately lost the auction on November 18 to Citadel's CEO Ken Griffin for $43 million. While ConstitutionDAO still had available funds remaining, they told members they didn't have sufficient funds to "insure, store, and transport the document."

Unfortunately for ConstitutionDAO, the real-time streaming of cumulative funds raised—the same tool they used to recruit new members—publicized their bid limit to their competitors. This presented other contenders with ample time to prepare a counter-bid strategy.

Although unsuccessful, their attempt onboarded many new people to crypto, promoted the concept of shared digital ownership, and will likely inspire other DAOs to participate in auctions of physical items in the future.

Beyond ConstitutionDAO and PleasrDAO, other prominent examples of collector DAOs include Flamingo, SquiggleDAO, BeetsDAO, Whale, MUSED, JennyDAO, and MeetbitsDAO.

Acquisition DAOs

Acquisition DAOs are groups designed to purchase and operate existing organizations such as sporting clubs, golf courses, or private companies through distributed voting and capital-raising. While this category of DAO has fewer existing case studies, this is set to change in the not-so-distant future.

Krause House (named after the former Chicago Bulls general manager Jerry Krause), for instance, raised USD $1.7 million in ETH in 2021 as part of its plan to purchase multiple basketball clubs in the future. The DAO plans to realize its goal by purchasing clubs in the G League (the NBA's developmental league), the NBL (Australia and New Zealand's pro league), and the WNBA (Women's National Basketball Association). The actual purchase of a major league club, though, will need strong cooperation from traditional and centralized organizations governing the relevant league in order for their ambitious road map to become a reality.

Another example is SeaWorld DAO, which hopes to pool funds to buy the SeaWorld theme park in Orlando, Florida, and is raising funds through NFT sales.[15]

Media DAOs

As the media companies of the web3 age, media DAOs communicate in writing, video streaming, audio, and social media and sometimes rally under the moniker Decentralized Autonomous Media Network (DAMN).

Media DAOs help to ensure that content is globally accessible and curated while giving power and a voice to those who consume their content. Part of this process takes the form of incentivizing content contributions and open governance over what content topics to prioritize. Unlike traditional media companies, participants can shape decisions on topics to cover, pieces to write, and projects to follow while sharing the collective upside of the organization through token ownership.

In terms of monetization, media DAOs mostly use web3 native methods. This includes NFTs, crowdfunding, and token sales in combination with traditional methods including paywalls, advertisements, and sponsored articles.

Examples of media DAOs include Forefront, Bankless, GCR, Darkstar, and rekt.

Philanthropic & Social Change DAOs

Philanthropic and social change DAOs seek to solve important issues and decentralize the governance of their operations through voting and grassroots proposals on a global scale. Token holders possess the power to choose for themselves how the future actions of the group are determined and what projects should be funded. The DAO format also adds additional transparency around how groups use members' donations as each transaction can be viewed and tracked on the blockchain, which helps to minimize fraud and unscrupulous behavior and facilitate analysis of the organization's efficacy.

---

[15] Note that it is difficult to discern the seriousness of this DAO's intent at the time of writing.

In addition, a DAO structure helps donations reach their intended audience by lowering inefficient administration costs and overheads incurred by middle layers of management, office space, and processing fees paid to multiple banks to transfer funds into regions with underserved financial infrastructure.

YellowHeart, cofounded by the band Maroon 5, is an example of a DAO formed to take collective actions towards social impact. Through the sale of music, art, events, and other NFT collectibles, YellowHeart raises money to finance initiatives voted on by its community members.

Another exciting development is play-to-earn DAOs, which offer a new paradigm for helping people to improve their economic circumstances. Arising from the technical and financial barriers of entry to play popular blockchain-based games such as Axie Infinity, DAOs including Yield Guild Games (YGG) and humanDAO have been established to level the playing field.

Leveraging new and emerging forms of online earning in the metaverse and play-to-earn gaming, HumanDAO provides income for members in underserved markets. Their north star is to support and empower members by enabling them to earn multiples on the income they would normally receive from traditional work in the real world.

To achieve their goal, humanDAO is providing educational resources and training on web3, cryptocurrency, the metaverse, and gaming strategy while lending game assets to those who cannot afford to purchase the NFT assets needed to play. The recipients of these assets and training can retain up to 70% of their in-game earnings, while the remainder is distributed to the managers (15%) who trained the players and to the DAO's treasury (15%).

HumanDAO will use this revenue stream to fund micro-lending projects, DAO projects, and community outreach in partnership with organizations including the United Nations World Food Programme (WFP) to provide meals for people in need. As with other DAOs, members can submit proposals to a vote and those that are successfully approved are funded by the DAO's treasury.

Other examples of DAOs active in the social change space include Charity DAO (crypto and blockchain applications for charitable giving), ChangeDAO (decentralized infrastructure for raising funds to drive social change), Citizen DAO (promotion of the UN sustainable development goals), and VitaDAO (healthcare research).

Environmental DAOs

Few causes rely on global participation and consensus as much as environmental change. DAOs offer an ideal structure to unite people across borders—while bypassing governments—to form a grassroots movement, action plan, or economy and then implement those tactics on the blockchain.

KlimaDAO, for instance, was created to tokenize carbon emissions as part of a token economy, with every KLIMA token backed by 1 tonne of verified carbon reduction or removal. Their goal is to accelerate the price appreciation of carbon assets as a tactic to incentivize companies and economies to pursue low-carbon technologies and carbon-removal projects.

Other examples of environment-focused DAOs include GreenClimateDAO and ClimateDAO.

6

BEST PRACTICES IN DAO DESIGN

While it's easy to start believing that every organization needs to be decentralized and autonomous, this is not true and there are many exceptions where a traditional organization format remains advantageous. This includes organizations that deal with decisions, projects, and transactions that don't take place on the public blockchain. This might take the form of an organization carrying out aged care or an organization that needs to stay highly local and accessible to non-tech savvy contributors, such as a school's parent group. Additionally, not all organizations value programmability, crypto, decentralization, and autonomy.

In general, a DAO structure works best for initiatives that want to connect and unify a diverse and dispersed group of people who don't know one another but who trust technology. In such cases, the DAO format helps to enforce trust, build group consensus, and align incentives between individuals who would otherwise not trust each other or work effectively in a group setting.

To start a new DAO, you can post an open proposal that describes your idea for a decentralized organization or software protocol, distribute voting tokens to potential contributors, and then launch the project once a majority vote is reached. Service DAOs such as Aragon offer a DAO deployment platform that you can leverage to initialize a DAO, including raising funds, issuing tokens, creating votes, and establishing governance protocols.

Beyond tooling options, you will need to put careful thought into the design of the DAO. This chapter intends to highlight specific design solutions and best practices for designing a DAO.

1) Inclusiveness

While DAOs are often gated by a financial threshold that necessitates the purchase of tokens or NFTs, most DAOs adhere to an inclusive membership policy with no specific identity required to be part of the community. In practice, most DAOs don't care how old you are, what you look like, or where you're from. In fact, they will probably never know. Once you have the tokens, NFTs, or invitation to sign in, you are automatically accepted into the community. Likewise, you don't need a work permit, visa, university diploma, or even fulfill a mandatory age requirement in order to participate. This digital guarantee offers three important advantages for decentralized organizations.

First, anyone with an Internet connection can join and participate in a DAO regardless of their age, nationality, or other personal traits that might limit their opportunity to participate in traditional organizations in the physical world. It is worth mentioning, here, that there are some exceptions. Zebpay, for instance, is a women-only DAO that aims to address and bypass unfair legacy systems by allowing women to compete on a level playing field for resources and decision-making.[16]

Second, few or no restrictions regarding who can join means that the organization has no limits on how large it can grow. This is important for DAOs with ambitious financial, philanthropic, political, or cultural goals.

Third, DAOs can be designed in such a way that respects pseudonymity and allows members to keep their nationality, race, age, gender, and other information private.

2) Transparency

While DAOs are transparent by nature—in that anyone can inspect past data and actions at any time—there needs to be an easy way to share and digest information. If full transparency depends on altruistic members sifting through Etherscan to cross-analyze past transactions and digging

---

[16] The DAO is planning to empower women in rural India by assisting groups to set up solar panels for mining Bitcoin.

through multiple group chats, poor treasury and project management practices can still carry on unnoticed.

This is why it's vital to organize and summarize information that takes place on the blockchain using traditional reports including an income statement, balance sheet, and operating expenses. To minimize human manipulation or interpretation errors, and ensure that reports are consistent with on-chain data, some DAOs use third-party software like Dune Analytics for building reports and live dashboards.

Olympus DAO, in the DeFi space, for example, has a live dashboard with key metrics placed prominently on its web application. This provides greater transparency into the health of the DAO's treasury assets, risk exposure, liquidity and other metrics. This, in turn, makes it easier to identify poor practices, disturbances in the financial well-being of the organization, volatility, or future vulnerabilities.

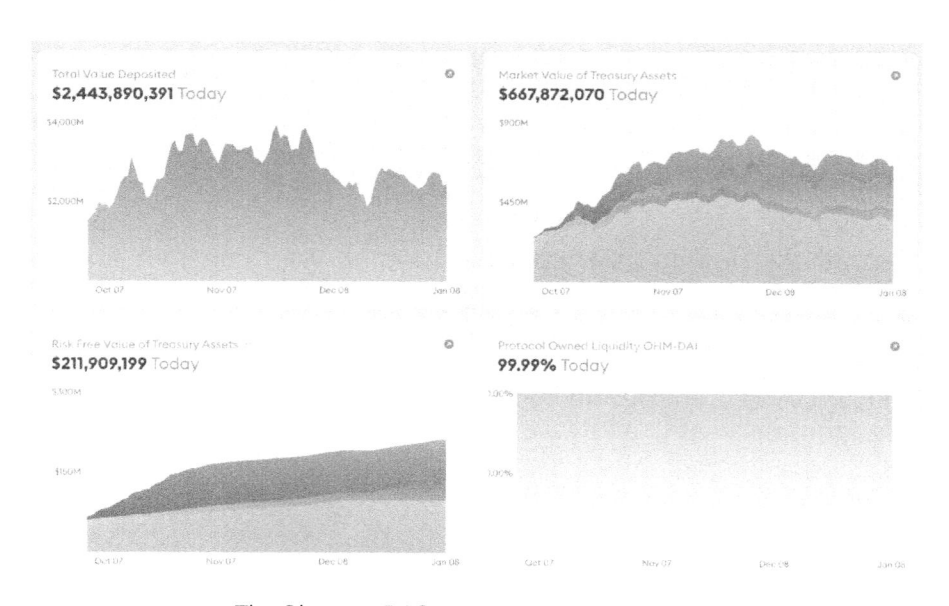

The Olympus DAO treasury asset dashboard

In the DeFi sector, the main threat to a DAO is financial risk. Explanatory tools are henceforth needed for members of the DAO to regularly monitor that risk, while also helping proxy voters (members who delegate their voting rights to another member) to assess the performance of their proxies in managing that risk.[17]

Transparency also becomes increasingly important as the DAO grows and matures. As the DAO takes on more projects, understanding the organization becomes incrementally complex and the learning curve for new members steepens as a result. Synthesizing past projects and buried records into a more digestible format (using visual metrics) makes it easier for new members to onboard and participate in a more meaningful way while helping the organization to scale beyond its original founding members.

The third benefit of adding quantitative tools and reports to the DAO's transparency stack is that it helps to create a flywheel for better decision-making. Explanatory graphics, for example, help to explain proposals or visualize risk to stakeholders who may not be technical financial experts and don't know how to vote on complex topics such as reducing collateral requirements or increasing token supply. By using visual tools, better decisions can accrue and compound, leading to better decision-making and outcomes with every vote.

3) Multi-step Governance

DAOs often follow a multi-step governance decision model where every decision needs to be approved by active users (e.g. 51%) before it can be activated or pushed to a final vote. There are several reasons for this mechanism. First, it disincentives spamming of proposals as you need to spend resources (in the form of tokens) in order to make a proposal active. Second, there is no associated risk for users who don't want to spend DAO resources/time on a project with little support. Third, it fosters a decentralized culture of decision-making, which is resilient since it doesn't depend on a single actor or group of actors. It can be used to make unbiased decisions even if the founders/developers leave the organization.

4) Proof-of-stake Voting

---

[17] Tarun Chitra, "Building and Running a DAO: Why Governance Matters", *future.a16z.com*, November 3, 2021.

While it may differ with each organization, a consensus-based proof-of-stake voting model generally provides a low barrier to vote by allowing anyone who holds tokens to participate in the DAO's governance system.

Proof-of-stake means that you need to prove you own a certain quantity of tokens in order for your vote to count. In this way, proof-of-stake liberates members from expending effort within the organization to gain voting rights (proof-of-work) and avoids the problem of established members centralizing the power.

New members can come in at any stage and enjoy the same level of input as established members—provided they invest sufficient capital and "skin in the game" by purchasing the native governance token. Proof-of-stake also maximizes the percentage of people who can vote, as there are typically more token holders than actively working token holders.

Finally, members who are actively contributing to the DAO will inherently accumulate tokens as a reward for their contribution and thereby have a voice in decision-making regardless.

5) Diverse and Open Initiatives

Members should have the option to participate based on their interests, with different initiatives founded and led by different parties within the DAO. This means that members can create or join initiatives according to their own desire without having to worry about conflicting agendas—and less need for voting wars between parties who have different project goals.

6) Caps on Proposals

While not always applicable, DAOs sometimes need to balance the need for users to express their ideas regarding the value of new proposals without strangle-holding the organization with incessant votes and proposals.

To demonstrate, proposals per member might need to be limited by a time period, meaning that it is not possible to spam the community with one weak proposal after another. Each proposal requires an upfront cost (not necessarily financially) to be activated so that the act of spamming does not benefit due to the high costs/complexity involved. This could come in the form of a quota system and a restriction on newly joined members making a proposal within their first month.

7) Internal Reputation

A member ranking system based on both reputation and past performance can help to facilitate quick evaluation and decision-making. Reputation is useful because it presents a way for people to judge if someone can be trusted without relying solely on information provided by others (a common problem with many social platforms) and provides a good measure for future trustworthiness.

Past performance is important as it allows DAOs to mitigate attempts of vote manipulation from single actors who aim only at benefiting themselves (i.e. recommending a service provider they own) and not the DAO. While it's still possible for bad actors to gain reputation and abuse that power, there is a strong disincentive mechanism or cost that will deter most people from trying.

8) Multi-level Wallet System

A multi-level wallet system helps re-establish control for token holders by splitting the right to spend tokens across multiple actors (with each actor holding a different part of the key). This way, an individual would need all private keys in order to move funds—making large token pools more secure even though they are collectively owned by many people.

While most DAO's tolerate or even embrace pseudonymity, including pseudonymous founders, insisting on identity or real-name verification for multi-sig holders may become more standard practice for DAOs managing large reserves of capital. This can help to prevent one individual from managing multiple pseudonymous identities (i.e. using multiple addresses and Discord identities) and collusion between wallet signees who know they can't be easily traced. For DeFi DAOs, the community may also like to assess the credentials of selected treasury managers, including their past work experience and criminal record (if any).

9) Register in a DAO-friendly Location

Next, it's worth watching the regulatory environment around establishing a DAO.

On June 28th 2021, the U.S. state of Wyoming legally recognized DAOs by granting them the same rights as limited liability companies, making Wyoming the first state in the US to do so. In fact, prior to this announcement, no formal legal recognition of DAOs existed anywhere in the world.

Besides not registering as a legal entity, DAOs traditionally established an offshore legal presence in countries such as Panama and the Cayman Islands, which are tax neutral, or incorporated as an onshore foundation in countries such as Switzerland and Singapore, which reduce legal liability. Additionally, some DAOs mixed and matched between two jurisdictions, such as Panama and Switzerland, which offers tax protection while at the same time shielding against legal liability. Still, no country or jurisdiction formally recognized DAOs as a unique legal entity.

The Wyoming DAO law now effectively allows DAOs, managed either by human members/managers or algorithmically, to conduct business in the state of Wyoming as a limited liability company (LLC). For DAOs, this unlocks several new benefits.

First, the new law empowers the state's judicial system to recognize smart contracts and blockchain records as legitimate proof of transfer, ownership, and operations. This makes it easier for DAO members to verify their voting history, transaction records, and decision-making process in a court of law.

Second, and perhaps more importantly, the new law makes it possible for DAO members to enjoy limited liability status. Under current laws, other jurisdictions in the U.S. and around the world could interpret DAO members as "partners" as part of a common-law partnership.[18] Such conditions mean that the personal assets of an individual DAO member are susceptible to lawsuit settlements and liabilities.

The new Wyoming DAO Law provides DAO members with the same limits to individual liability offered to members of limited liability companies. By formalizing limited liability for DAO members and protecting their rights as legal persons in state

---

[18] Andrew Bull, "Regulators Everywhere Should Follow Wyoming's DAO Law", *Coin Desk*, July 9, 2021.

court, this law helps to remove ambiguity and alleviate the concern of individuals who may otherwise be held personally liable simply by forming or participating in a DAO.

It's important to note that while a DAO can be registered as an LLC in a jurisdiction such as Wyoming, the founders of a DAO are still vulnerable to violating securities law by promoting a token to unaccredited investors. While there remains legal uncertainty, especially with the lack of precedent cases, it is possible that DAOs could obtain the same status as Bitcoin or Ethereum, which are not currently regarded as a security by the U.S. Securities and Exchange Commission (SEC). This is given on the grounds that there is no substantive control by any one person or centralized group within these projects, as decision-making is diffused across a network of participants.[19]

Third, the new law creates crucial momentum for legal recognition, and Wyoming's history for innovation in corporate legal innovation is not lost on DAO advocates like Andrew Bull (a founding partner of Bull Blockchain Law) who call for further recognition and innovation.

In 1977, Wyoming became the first state in the U.S. to recognize the LLC structure, which combined the limited shareholder liability of a corporation with the informal decision procedures of a partnership. The LLC structure later became adopted by the IRS for tax purposes as well as other states and countries.

Bull is hoping that like the intellectual currency of an LLC, other jurisdictions and countries will follow Wyoming's lead in creating a new legal structure and taxation law specific for DAOs, including U.S. Congress and the European Union. According to Bull, "Wyoming's DAO law lays the first brick on a long path towards a complete regulatory framework and widespread acceptance for DAOs."[20]

10) Hiring

---

[19] While not proven, the founders of Decentraland, for example, may have stepped back their involvement from the project to push Decentraland towards a fully decentralized organization in order to avoid regulatory attention.

[20] Andrew Bull, "Regulators Everywhere Should Follow Wyoming's DAO Law", *Coin Desk*, July 9, 2021.

After building up a large community and treasury balance, it's important for a DAO to hire talent to manage and secure those resources, perform administration tasks, support community initiatives, and manage other day-to-day operations. DAOs who fail to hire and reward contributors for their work are at a greater risk of exposing themselves to critical security risks and becoming threadbare in terms of active participation.

Hiring itself can be directed towards task-based work or full-time positions, such as a full-time blockchain developer or community manager. While elements of centralization are impossible to avoid, such as access to the multi-sig wallet and treasury security management, the general rule of hiring is to keep everything open and transparent. This means hiring by group consensus, where positions are opened to the community and the community can vote on an appropriate candidate to hire.

By the same token, this process can be applied to intervene and potentially relieve a member who is not fulfilling their duties. TributeDAO, which develops smart contract architecture for other DAOs, has a Guild Kick policy that provides a formal process to kick out a member from the DAO for any given reason. For someone to be removed, the other members of the DAO must submit a proposal. If the proposal passes a vote, the member in question will be subsequently removed and permitted to withdraw their funds (based on what they held when the kickout process began).

11) Treasury Management

Like a traditional company, it's vital for DAOs to manage their assets and capital as their treasury expands[21] (including native tokens or other holdings such as Ether). As Tarun Chitra of Gauntlet Network notes, "corporate governance best practices lend themselves well to DAOs."[22]

Diversification, for example, is an important consideration given that most DAOs have low asset diversification and a large part of their treasury held in their native governance

---

[21] As of late 2021, the top 20 DAOs alone manage over USD $14 billion in assets.
[22] Tarun Chitra, "Building and Running a DAO: Why Governance Matters", *future.a16z.com*, November 3, 2021.

token—and a volatile asset class at that! Consider, for example, the effect on the DAO's balance sheet if the native governance token suddenly dropped 50 percent. Without proper diversification, this event would not only undermine the DAO's capacity to weather a market downturn but also its ability to finance day-to-day operations and long-term projects.

This is why it's recommended that DAOs pursue diversification strategies and potentially hire professional treasury managers. These measures help to ensure the DAO can adequately fund core development and upcoming initiatives such as a merger and acquisition (M&A), token buyback, or new project funding.

One industry-standard approach is to allocate part of the treasury's holdings in stablecoins to cover 12-24 months of operating expenses. This strategy provides more financial resilience in the event of a sudden market crash or an extended downturn because unlike other cryptocurrencies, stablecoins are designed to withstand volatility. By pegging their market value to an external reference asset such as US dollars, gold, or the price of another commodity, stablecoins achieve price stability using collateralization or algorithmic mechanisms to buy and sell the reference asset.

On top of stability, stablecoins can be deposited into DeFi platforms to earn interest by providing liquidity for secured loans to other parties. These returns can be as high as 12% a year (as of late 2021) on platforms such as Yearn, Aave, BlockFi, Gemini, and Compound. Additionally, stablecoins are a practical medium of exchange for rewarding contributors or distributing grants to members.

Beyond stablecoins, there are cryptocurrency-based ETPs (exchange-traded products) including Index Coop and the Bankless BED Index that allow DAOs to gain broad exposure to different sectors or underlying themes across different markets.

In some instances, a DAO's treasury may decide to hold governance tokens from other DAOs (with a shared vision) as a way to positively support and influence the sector as well as build cooperation and cohesion across organizations. Of course, there is also the possibility that some DAOs may exploit this ability to hold governance rights in other DAOs as a way to intervene in the affairs of those organizations.

12) Key Performance Indicators

Just like a traditional organization, it's important to continuously monitor the wellbeing of a DAO, incentivize performance, and reward over-achievement by tracking various key performance indicators (KPIs).

To operate effectively, KPIs should be clearly defined and publicly verifiable. KPI tracking can usually be added to the DAO's technology stack via adding a new software solution or installing a plugin. Key performance indicators typically include the percentage of active contributors, contributors retained after three months, and the time between joining and the first contribution as part of the DAO's onboarding and conversion funnel.

KPIs also need to be fixed to the DAO's treasury to ensure the organization can meet its financial goals. For example, "Can the DAO survive a 90% crash in asset prices?" or "Can the DAO continue to afford to purchase high-ticket NFTs based on the interest earned on its holdings?" Specific metrics might include planned versus actual expenditure, 12-month runway, diversification index, and the ratio of stablecoins to other cryptocurrencies.

Governance, meanwhile, can be tracked by monitoring the voting participation rate and proposal approval rate, which will help to pinpoint potential problems such as long-term voter apathy, skewed voting patterns (i.e. based on time zones or year of joining the DAO), and unsuccessful proposals that failed due to low voter turnout. Of note, voter participation tends to fall as DAOs scale in size. As highlighted by Dan Wu of Orca, appromiately 75% of Compound (a major DeFi DAO) token holders have never participated in an on-chain governance proposal despite being eligible to vote.[23]

---

[23] Dan Wu, "Governance Participation: Perils and Promise", *orca.mirror.xyz*, January 7, 2022.

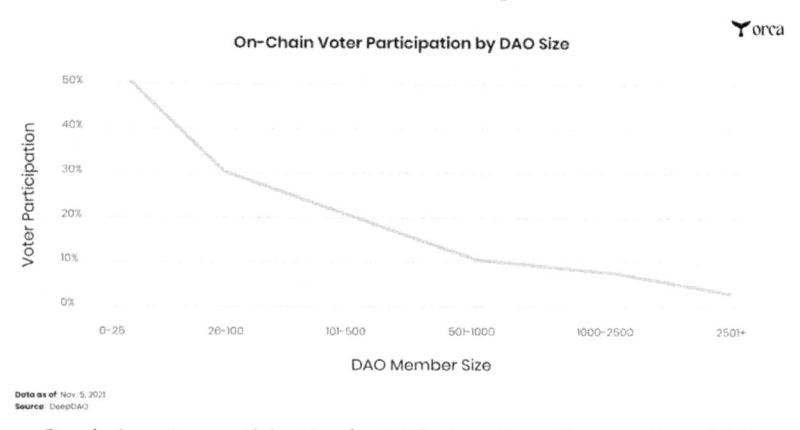

On-chain voter participation by DAO size, Orca, Source: DeepDAO

Capitalizing on the diversity and wisdom of the crowd is a core advantage of a DAO's setup. Hence, as much as possible, governance and voting should be an organization-wide undertaking and not an activity for a selected few. In this way, a Gini index/ratio may need to be established to measure the statistical dispersion of native token ownership among members and identify inequality, as this may be the cause of voting patterns. The index of native token ownership is a key metric as it helps to identify or explain voter patterns, especially if voting is weighted according to the number of tokens each member holds.

In DAOs where the tokens are inefficiently distributed and voting is weighted, it's only natural that participants with the highest number of tokens are the one's incentivized to vote, which may help to explain voter apathy and attrition, as the vote of most members has little impact on the future direction of the DAO.

13) Scaling Challenges

Size of the network is part and parcel of success in the digital era but there are also scaling problems that come with a growing membership. Large DAOs also inevitably face unique problems that smaller DAOs do not. These challenges include coordination and communication friction, an over-run of activity, and a declining sense of community based on

Dunbar's number of 150 people, which is the suggested cognitive limit for maintaining stable social relationships.

This growth trap is acute for DAOs that follow an open membership policy where the success of the organization generates attention and begets more new members. This leaves large or fast-growing DAOs susceptible to collapsing under the gravity of their own success.

Countermeasures for tackling this problem include hiring full-time coordination managers, partitioning the DAO into sub-DAOs, and potentially even forking the DAO into two or more DAOs. A more contentious solution is to raise the bar for entry into the DAO by raising the cost to participate, as explored in the next section.

Finally, a vote delegation option might be needed as DAOs scale, especially as data shows that voter participation as a percentage falls as membership of the DAO grows. Vote delegation can be implemented using tools such as Sybil, which gives members the ability to stand as a delegate or delegate their vote(s) to other members. Representative leadership vis-à-vis vote delegation is also useful for votes on highly technical decisions, such as treasury management practices.

14) Exclusivity

One of the biggest decisions when designing a DAO comes with the trade-off between exclusivity and openness. Exclusivity, in the form of restricting access to a DAO or a limit on who can participate, raises the desirability of the organization and the value of the DAO's native token. A cap on the number of participants also keeps the organization at a size that is easier to manage.

Open membership, on the other hand, enables anyone to join. This can help to raise the public profile and reach of the organization but can also create more chaos and demand more effort to manage and adequately engage members.

Some DAOs innately benefit from open membership, such as ConstitutionDAO, which accepted cryptocurrency contributions from members in an effort to outbid a billionaire for an original copy of the United States' Constitution auctioned at Sotheby's in late 2021. Each new member of the DAO effectively added to the pool of available capital, which created an incentive to keep the barrier of entry low. Open membership also fulfilled the DAO's mission of distributing ownership of the U.S. Constitution to the public. Conversely, a social DAO might (that centers on discussion and maybe operates as a private chat group) value gated access or exclusivity and only accepts interesting individuals whose ideas and ethos align with the group's mission.

While barriers of entry will differ from one DAO to the next, there has been a growing trend towards higher barriers of entry—especially as DAOs become more established. This is evidenced by the high upfront cost of participating in a DAO via ownership of the DAO's native token. While this requirement is necessary for investment-based DAOs that co-invest in large projects, the financial requirements are less obvious for non-investment DAOs. To participate in the Friends With Benefits DAO, a participant must own 75 $FWB tokens, which as of late 2021 costs USD $60 per token ($5,400 in total).

While financial barriers help to control the number of entrants and simplify community management, such barriers clash with the openness expounded by web3 to level the playing field between platforms and individuals.

The problem also deepens when it comes to managing token economics. As DAOs are valued based on the price of their native token, there's an inherent incentive to inflate the value of the token. DAOs can manipulate the value of their token in two ways. The first is to increase market demand by increasing the cost of entry to their DAO, i.e. from 100 tokens to 200 tokens. For highly-desired DAOs, this is an easy way to increase the demand for its native token.

The second option is to reduce the pool of available tokens on the open market by utilizing the DAO's treasury to purchase and lock up more of its native tokens to reduce the available supply. Both actions effectively increase the cost of entry for new participants based on a reduction in supply or increase in demand for the DAO's native token.

DAOs are cognisant of this dilemma and the culture they set by carrying out such policies. For DAOs that are not strictly vehicles for investment, an alternative option is to remove all barriers to entry. This, though, affects the desirability of the organization as participation is no longer exclusive and a flood of new members may not be in the interest of fulfilling the DAO's mandate.

Another solution is to create tiers of membership, as both Friends With Benefits and the BanklessDAO provide. While Full Membership of Friends With Benefits requires 75 tokens, a Local Membership only costs 5 tokens, which offers limited access to Discord channels but the same access to offline events as a Full Membership.

A more promising solution, however, is a transition proposed by Gaby Goldberg from a membership model based on financial proof to a new model based on past contributions.[24] At present, the barrier to participation is based on what you own (in the form of tokens) as this is simple and easy to verify on-chain. The DAO's online interface can simply scan someone's Ethereum address and validate if they qualify to participate based on the specific tokens or NFTs they hold. In the future, rather than assess what a new member owns on the Ethereum, Solana, or other blockchain, more DAOs might assess what a new participant has contributed in the past based on on-chain records of their work.

Similar to a digital resume, individuals will be able to accumulate an on-chain history and record of their contributions using third-party tools such as Rabbithole that track their contributions made to other DAOs or digital projects.

Digital records not only help DAOs to find participants who have a proven track record and a relevant skillset but also incentivize individuals to contribute. As participants earn equity tokens by completing tasks, they are able to enhance their digital resume, future earning capacity, and value on the labor market.

For now, though, exclusivity is a key problem that remains unresolved. Many critics of web3 already fear a world of more exclusive groups based on more exclusive assets. As mentioned, this conflicts with the promise of web3 to create equal opportunity to access assets, people, resources, and information.

---

[24] Gaby Goldberg, "Social Token Complex", August 2021, https://gaby.mirror.xyz/zqchiBQhWWS49gaabLU92-BUUwfBL5aHCtNT88VTI8o

A negative perception of DAOs as exclusive clubs may also be compounded by negative activities including pumping and dumping assets and other forms of market manipulation that could draw added criticism to decentralized organizations. As DAOs attract adoption and more mainstream attention, how they react and balance exclusivity and openness in their ranks will be a key battlefield for debate in the coming years.

7

STARTING YOUR OWN JOURNEY

With freelance contracts gaining pace at replacing full-time positions in the labor market, fewer people expect to have a job for life. This trend, converging with the evolution of DAOs and project-based work environments, is the fulfillment of what the authors of *The Sovereign Individual: Mastering the Transition to the Information Age* call a labor system allotted into "tasks", "not jobs" as part of a new arrangement of hire.

DAOs, though, even disrupt the recent gig economy because while work is often compensated on a task-by-task basis, the equity of the organization is shared among all actors in the network rather than siloed by centralized companies like Uber and Fiverr.

The emergence of DAOs also helps to fill the void left by traditional unions to protect workers' rights by allowing all workers to coordinate and vote on strategies that combat unfair work. DAOs too can potentially provide health insurance and other benefits, as highlighted in this chapter.

Going Full-time

In 2021, Cooper Turley made the announcement that he was working full-time for a collection of DAOs. Publishing on his Mirror channel, Cooper writes, "The world is changing. We can work on what we love, and get paid in the process. Today - I'm going full-time on DAOs."[25]

Cooper started his journey with DAOs in 2018. He began by writing external content for MetaCartel and Moloch to share the message of those two DAOs and earn governance tokens in order to participate in their governance platforms. From

---

[25] Cooper Turnley, "Full-time DAOs", *Coopahtroopa*, September 10 2021, https://coopahtroopa.mirror.xyz

there, Cooper focused on drafting internal on-chain proposals and creating templates for community decisions.

He has gone on to contribute to over 20 DAOs including PleasrDAO and Audius. Part of Cooper's success has been his ability to take his learnings from one DAO community to another and create templates to "reduce, reuse and recycle time and energy".[26]

Cooper concedes that as a full-time participant in a collection of DAOs, he foregoes traditional compensation, including a fixed salary, healthcare benefits, and a 401k. He instead relies on tokens, which confer him equity and upside in the potential growth of each DAO. At the same time, he doesn't receive any compensation for his work in fiat currency. Instead, he is paid primarily in ETH and USDC, which are converted from his earned governance tokens.

Cooper writes in a blog post, "My challenge is finding productive ways to put those tokens to work so that I can sustain myself without having to liquidate tokens."[27]

While reliance on DAOs for financial income can be challenging in terms of managing non-salary benefits including medical insurance and retirement funds, new solutions are on the way to cater to the emerging labor market and the demands of the sovereign individual. Leveraging the economics of group purchase, a DAO called Opolis, for example, provides health, dental, and vision insurance, as well as group 401(k), solo 401(k), and various IRA options for DAOs to support their contributors and attract new members.

Finding a DAO

Similar to finding work as a freelancer in the gig economy, you will need to be highly proactive and seek out opportunities to become involved in one or more DAOs. Unlike full-time employment, there are no limits on participating in multiple organizations. While Cooper has found success participating in multiple DAOs, he has noted in media interviews that new entrants should focus their efforts on one

---

[26] Cooper Turnley, "Full-time DAOs", *Coopahtroopa*, September 10 2021, https://coopahtroopa.mirror.xyz
[27] Cooper Turnley, "Full-time DAOs", *Coopahtroopa*, September 10 2021, https://coopahtroopa.mirror.xyz

or two DAOs to maximize their contributions, especially early on in their DAO career. At the same time, focusing on one DAO and not overcommitting leaves the door open to working full-time for one DAO in the future.

As illustrated in the previous chapter, there is already a vast number of active DAOs providing solutions across a diverse spread of sectors. One of the biggest factors when choosing the right DAO is whether you want to earn equity through labor contributions or put your existing funds to work through an equity contribution.

In the case of the latter, you could join a DAO like Neon DAO that allows you to co-invest in metaverse projects after making a minimal contribution of 60 ETH to the DAO's investment pool. In the case of the former, rather than making an upfront investment of funds, you are instead offering your time and effort (sweat equity) in order to acquire equity in the form of tokens. The Aragon Court DAO, for instance, rewards contributors by participating in disputes that require human judgment. The concept is similar to jury duty in the real world except you can do everything online and get paid for it in the form of tokens.

To be eligible to participate as a Guardian in the Aragon Court, you will first need to purchase the Aragon token called ANT (min. of 100 tokens as of 2021). After you have staked the minimal amount of ANT, you will be eligible to adjudicate a dispute and cast your vote as a Guardian. If you perform certain actions on time (after reviewing the information provided), you will earn token rewards in return for your contribution. Note that the ability to be summoned to a dispute (and therein earn a reward) is directly proportional to the amount of ANT that you have staked in the system. Additionally, you can earn subscription fees for being an active Guardian on the platform, regardless of whether or not you are summoned. You can assign your availability within the Aragon Court dashboard, which you can log into instantly using a MetaMask wallet.

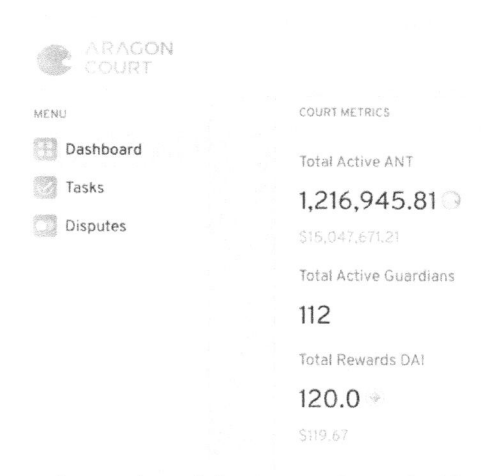

Screenshot of the Aragon Court dashboard

For those with a convenient Internet connection and an interest in justice, this is a great way to participate in a DAO—all without drafting proposals and navigating complex internal procedures. You also don't need any legal knowledge or background in order to participate.

Aragon, though, is just one DAO, and there are probably other DAOs that better align with your interests and relevant skillset. Like any career decision, it's important to take your time and explore different options before you commit to one organization. Your research should include sussing out the general vibe or culture of the community. People are what make a DAO special and an interesting place to work. So, try to see how members address each other and how they approach their work before you decide to join formally.

After finding a DAO that fits your interests and skills, you will need to find the core communication and coordination hub for that organization. This is usually Telegram, Discord, or a dashboard web application. After joining, you can find onboarding information and browse internal chats based on themes such as open proposals, memes, general chatter, and FAQs.

There's usually a designated area where new participants can inform the community about how they wish to contribute and what skills they have to offer. Examples of in-demand skills include computer programming, writing and content

65

production, analysis, meme art, legal services, and community management.

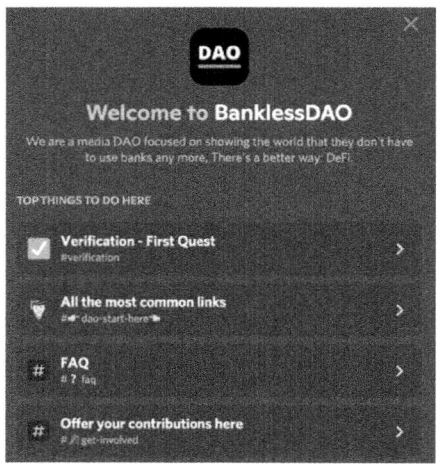

Onboarding message after joining the BanklessDAO Discord channel

New chat channels will sometimes be unlocked to you as you participate further in the DAO. Access stratification is used both as an incentive to participate and as a barrier to curate the community and shield groups who are accountable for key deliverables. The BanklessDAO has three levels of Discord channel access including Member (35,000 BANK), Contributor (35,000 BANK + Invitation by Genesis Team), and Whale (150,000 BANK).

To officially join a DAO such as Bankless or Friends With Benefits, you will need to buy their native token, called BANK (which has no value but offers governance participating rights) and $FWB respectively. After buying or receiving the native governance token, you will be eligible to vote and issue new proposals using an external platform such as Snapshot. Note that you will be required to connect your digital wallet (usually MetaMask) and verify your equity holdings in order to use web3 platforms such as Snapshot.

Before joining a DAO, it's also worth investigating that organization's exit policy, sometimes known in the DAO space as "rage quitting". Borrowed from gaming and general Internet parlance, rage quit refers to the process of hastily exiting a DAO when your values or level of commitment no longer align with the organization. While it will depend on the scope of the DAO, you should have the freedom to leave and take your tokens/funds with you, which therein enables you to quit in rage at any time.

Due to the dynamic nature of DAOs and the fluidity of contribution and collaboration, most DAOs expect members to leave, and, in fact, encourage unsatisfied or inactive members to free up space for new members. In some circumstances, it's possible for you to be removed from a subcommittee or an entire DAO through group consensus mechanisms, as mentioned in the last chapter. Note, too, that there are sometimes stricter exit conditions for investment DAOs that lock up contributors' investments for an agreed period of time.

Compensation Methods

Once you have chosen a DAO to join, you can start to investigate different ways to get involved. There any usually multiple options including work tasks, committee roles, grants programs, and bounties as we will explore in this section.

First, it's important to understand that working for a DAO can be a volatile source of income and it generally takes time and effort to get paid for your work, especially as some methods of compensation are based on the final output rather than on an upfront or hourly basis. In special cases, payment may even be issued retroactively.

Second, in the nascent DAO economy, there are few set standards and no regulated minimum wage for benchmarking how much contributors should be paid. Compensation depends on the size of the DAO's treasury, the value contributors deliver, and how the community values different skillsets or tasks.

How DAO's pay their contributors can vary too. Some DAOs pay a standard hourly rate, whereas other DAOs rely on tipping and peer-to-peer reward tools such as Coordinape that enable contributors to reward each other. There are also grants that contributors can apply for based on pre-defined projects as well as bounties with an upfront price tag.

Let's now review some of the most common methods for compensation.

Fixed Role

Established or well-funded DAOs usually offer fixed job roles in the areas of community coordination, treasury management, social media management, and onboarding that are based on a regular commitment over an extended period of time. Like a salary, fixed roles provide a relatively consistent and reliable source of income.

The specific payout or salary is usually determined through community voting and compensated on an hourly or weekly basis in the form of stablecoins and/or governance tokens. Under this model, the DAO—through its voting members—assumes the responsibility of fairly compensating contributors while balancing the need to incentivize contributions and preserve the treasury's balance. In other words, the community effectively accepts the risk of disproportionately compensating contributors relative to the actual output received.

According to the *DAOs: The New Coordination Frontier* report conducted by Gitcoin and the BanklessDAO in 2021, the primary sources of compensation for DAO contributors were community-based/peer-to-peer distribution (via Coordinape), project-based distribution, and bounties.

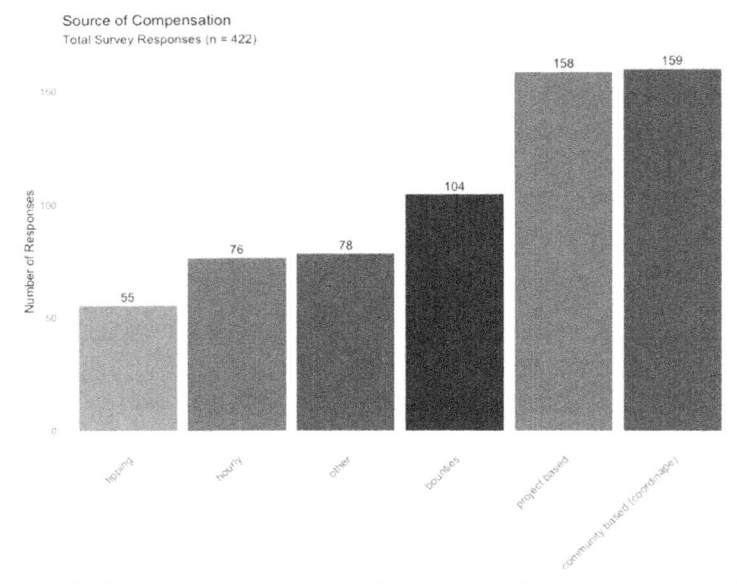

Sources of DAO compensation, *DAOs: The New Coordination Frontier* 2021 report

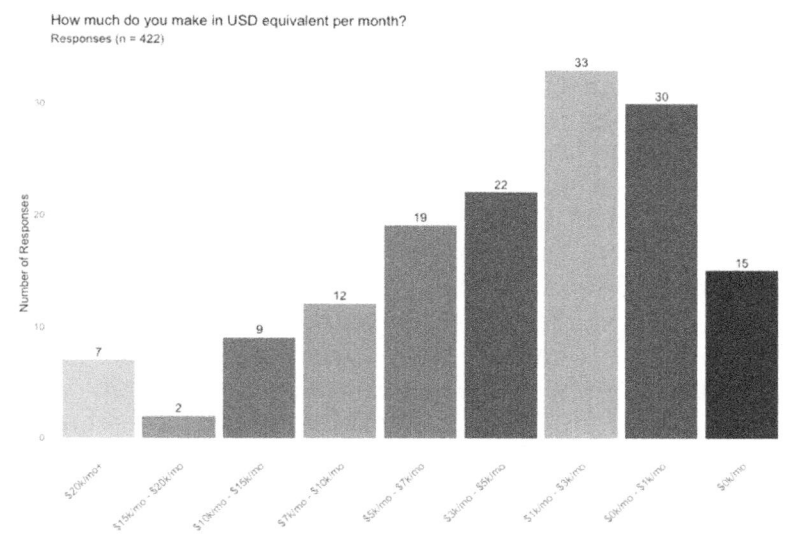

Monthly DAO income, *DAOs: The New Coordination Frontier* 2021 report

Furthermore, almost half of the respondents (189/422) reported that DAOs were not their primary source of income, while some respondents reported earning USD $5,000 to $10,000 per month (comparable or higher than a traditional salary in most cities).

Grants Program

After amassing large treasury holdings, many DeFi projects (including Compound, Aave, and Uniswap) and some virtual worlds (such as Decentraland and The Sandbox) design grants programs as a vehicle to attract special contributions. In the case of virtual worlds in the metaverse, grants can be received for creating events, games, and other projects that help attract attention to that given world. By submitting an application and perhaps even building an MVP (minimal viable project), applicants can receive funding to complete and deliver their product idea.

Bounty

Bounties provide a permissionless option of matching passions with one-off tasks. This remuneration method provides a fixed reward in return for a pre-defined work task. Security specialists, for example, can be rewarded for identifying vulnerabilities as part of a bug bounty reward offered by DeFi DAOs.

For individuals, bounties offer a frictionless way to support a DAO. They don't have to join a guild, participate in meetings, propose their services, or navigate chat groups and voting polls. The financial reward is clearly defined and distributed immediately upon the completion of the task as defined by the terms and conditions (coded in the smart contract).

For DAOs, bounties help attract talent from a different class of contributors (i.e. solo types). Market rates for bounties, though, can be expensive. In general, bounties only work for tasks with criteria that can be easily defined and evaluated.

Examples of DAOs providing bounties are Layer3, Immunefi, Balancer, and Gitcoin. Balancer offers 1,000 ETH to those who can expose critical bugs that might be exploited to drain their V2 Vault.

Tip/Bonus

Tipping or bonuses recognize spontaneous value creation. Under this compensation method, everyone has the potential to receive a reward for consistent and meaningful participation that falls outside the confines of other compensation methods such as bounty, fixed role, and grant program. While this method relies on some centralization and concentration of power, more and more DAOs are employing tools to tip members.

To overcome the problem of a central group or individual controlling the tips jar, there are tools such as Coordinape that provide a peer-to-peer tipping system that decentralizes the distribution of rewards. This type of peer-to-peer reward system—non-existent in traditional organizations—is becoming increasingly popular and introduces an internal economy of activity within the DAO that reinforces active participation, accountability, and responsibility.

Retroactive Payment

Finally, contributors can issue a request to be paid for tasks completed. While this form of compensation is more flexible and initially permissionless (i.e. you don't need to wait for approval to get started), there's no guarantee that you will actually get paid! What's more, you still need to navigate the DAO's bureaucracy and permission system to receive a retroactive payment. Retroactive compensation, though, can be a good last resort for completed work that doesn't fit into other categories of compensation.

How to Participate

The transition from joining to actively participating in a DAO usually takes time and a lot of energy before you start to see results. In addition, many DAO contributors report being initially overwhelmed by the sheer amount of information, activity, and complex taxonomy of group chats and guilds. While it's natural to try and keep up with everything that is happening, this is a sure way to overload and prematurely burn yourself out.

Instead, it's best to find bounties, grants, groups, or guilds that align with your interests and skillset, such as security research, brand-building, or events. Also, don't be afraid to take your time and investigate what different groups are working on and their general vibe before you commit.

While you won't always be able to start contributing to a project right away, you can begin by following and contributing to the conversation in the discussion channels. After an intensive week or two of studying the group chat, documentation, checking the calendar, and understanding the group's objectives, you can start jumping into live meetings, brainstorming in chats, and seeking out opportunities to contribute to a task or project in any feasible way you can.

Unlike in the corporate world or the public sector, other members of the group won't sit you down (like your last supervisor) and help you plan out your first task. Instead, you have to be proactive and declare your availability or volunteer yourself for a specific task or project.

For tasks, you can usually get straight to work once you have permission from the group. An example of a task might be taking notes in the next meeting or translating the newsletter. For projects, you will need to present your proposal to the group at a meeting, clarify your idea in writing via a public forum or the discussion channel, and build (soft) consensus within the group.

Overall, you will need to work hard and be proactive and consistent at every stage, as again, no supervisor is breathing down your neck checking your progress and leading the way for you. This is freedom but it's also a responsibility. For this reason, it's practical to start by making small commitments before working your way up to participating in bigger projects or steering your own.

DAO Fatigue

As most participants still rely on a day job to sustain themselves and their family, and work takes place asynchronously in front of a screen, DAO fatigue can be a serious problem. For some people, the fast pace and reliance on group chats to keep up-to-date with everything that's happening as well as the sheer scope and magnitude of the DAO's work can prove stressful and overwhelming. Frustration with the level of engagement of less active contributors and divided opinions are other common sources of dissatisfaction.

Hence, while it might seem initially exciting to lead a double life between a DAO and a day job, it's valuable to play the long game and avoid burning out too early. If you live in an unfavorable time zone, you might need to rely on reading the meeting notes rather than participating in live calls, for example. Also, remember that, unlike a traditional job, there are lower costs to switching from one DAO to another. This means you can easily hop to a new DAO if the current DAO becomes unsustainable without upsetting your career resume, social status, or a supervisor who vouched for you two weeks ago.

Given the asymmetrical challenge of digital work on a global scale, it's essential as well that DAOs build tools, processes, and a contributor experience that respects mental health and doesn't overwhelm members. This is why it's practical that as a DAO scales, guilds/working committees and sub-DAOs are established to reduce the load on communication channels and streamline decision-making.

Removing redundant work, adding caps on voting proposals, and providing detailed onboarding materials and documentation to avoid repeated questions in group chats can also help to prevent compounding anxiety and free up mental space.

Finally, it's vital to automate as much work as possible, including reports and visualizations using third-party tools and to hire full-time contributors as much as possible.

8

HOW TO CREATE A DAO

Maybe you're itching to create a DAO but have no idea where to begin. A good first step is to become involved with an existing DAO in your field of interest and learn about the general experience of participating in a DAO from the perspective of a contributor.

The next step is to weigh up whether your vision for a new organization fits into a DAO structure. Will most of the organization's activities and transactions take place in the physical world or on the blockchain? How will your DAO generate income? Does your organization need to be tokenized? If the organization has no income, such as a meme group chat or a gardening club, then the upfront investment of setting up a multi-sig wallet, treasury, and governance tokens—on top of gas fees for using the Ethereum network— might not make financial sense.

In addition, there is a steep learning curve to overcome for people to participate effectively in a DAO. This includes an understanding of DAO terminology, tooling (i.e. MetaMask wallet and other software tools), processes, and token management. Therefore, you'll need to assess the ability of your target members to learn and operate in a decentralized and autonomous environment.

Once you feel confident with your understanding of DAOs, gained some first-hand experience, and feel sure that a DAO structure is an appropriate fit, then you can start to test the waters by drafting a mission statement and preparing the infrastructure for running a DAO.

1) Mission Statement

The first and perhaps most important step is to draft the DAO's mission statement, also known as a *manifesto*. This document introduces the DAO and states the goal of the DAO (what the organization is working to achieve) and why potential contributors should be reasonably motivated to join the organization. Google's mission, for example, is to organize the world's information and make it universally accessible and useful.

DAO	DAO Type	Goal
PleasrDAO	NFT Art Curation	Collect digital art that represents and funds important ideas.
ConstitutionDAO	Curation	Buy a copy of the U.S. Constitution.
FreeRossDAO	Advocacy	Free Ross Ulbricht, alleged founder of the Silk Road e-commerce site, from prison.
BanklessDAO	Media/Culture	Propagate crypto media and culture; help the world go bankless.
Friends With Benefits	Social/Culture	Push for a bright future; a world in which prosperity is abundant and technology acts as a communal connective tissue.
Klima DAO	Environment/Advocacy	Create a future where the cost of carbon to the climate is embedded into the economic system, through the creation and governance of a carbon-backed currency that aligns incentives between investors, civil society, and organizations.
Uniswap	DeFi	Build a future where anyone in the world can access financial services without fear of discrimination or counterparty risk.

Mission statements of popular DAOs

2) Governance

The next important step is to create a framework for governance and token distribution ownership to members. At this stage, you may like to recruit other founding members to help you design the DAO and distribute decision-making.

As discussed in Chapter 4, there are many ways to design DAO governance, including open governance, leadership/committee-based governance, and proxy-based governance. Typically, this decision will need to be made in accordance with the mission of the DAO, membership criteria, and the technical nature of the DAO and its member profile. If the DAO has an open membership policy and an inclusive mission statement, open governance may be an optimal framework. Meanwhile, DeFi DAOs that perform highly complicated tasks or rely on technical decision-making may need a proxy or leadership/committee-based governance model.

Decision-making itself can be implemented on-chain or off-chain. On-chain governance takes place through voting tied to tokens, whereas off-chain governance evolves through online discussions via chat apps, group calls, and forum posts. In both cases, forum proposals are generally created by a member or members of the DAO, and those that reach a soft consensus or a certain level of backing or popularity will be submitted for a vote to reach a hard consensus. If the vote fulfills minimum criteria, including quorum (minimum number of votes), the proposal will be passed and initiated.

3) Launching Your DAO

Once you have a mission statement and a preliminary governance framework, you are now ready to set up the infrastructure to launch a DAO.

In this section, we will explore a quick demonstration on how to set up a DAO on the Ethereum blockchain using the Aragon Client. While most DAOs currently operate on the Ethereum blockchain and most web3 tools run on this network, note that other blockchains may become more popular in the future.

Aragon, as covered in earlier chapters, offers a suite of open-source solutions for creating and managing a DAO, including Aragon Court for DAO dispute resolution mentioned in Chapter 7. Aragon currently offers two primary options for DAOs: **Aragon Client** and **Aragon Govern**. Aragon Client is the full-service solution suite, while Aragon Govern offers a set of governance plugins. While you will need to conduct your own research on how to establish a DAO entity that meets your needs, for this demonstration, we will select the Aragon Client option.

From aragon.org, click on the "**Create Your DAO**" button. This will trigger the following pop-up tab.

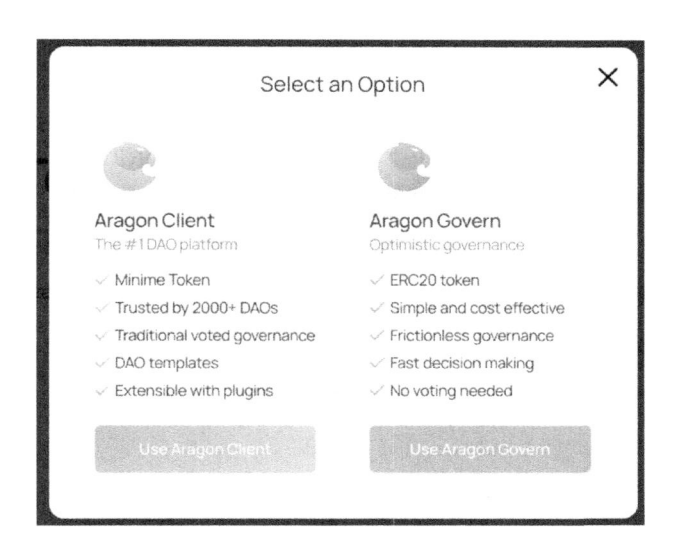

Next, you will be directed to a landing page where you can create a new organization or open an existing organization. From here, click on the first option to **Create an organization**.

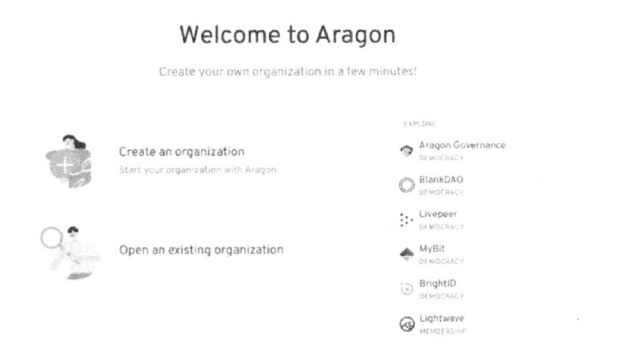

You can see sample DAO dashboards by clicking on the sample DAOs on the right

Next, you will be asked to connect to the Aragon web application using an Ethereum-based wallet. Aragon currently supports MetaMask, Frame, Fortmatic, and Portis. For this demonstration, we will use the MetaMask wallet. Please note that you can find instructions for installing a MetaMask wallet in the Appendix section of this book.

77

After installing and signing in to your MetaMask wallet, you will need to sign approval for the Aragon Client to connect to your wallet. In order to create a DAO, Aragon requires that you have at least 0.2 Ether in your wallet. Note that you can create a dummy DAO using the Rinkeby Test Network and simulation Ether. This means that you don't need to spend real Ether to create a practice account. You can borrow simulation Ether for use on the Rinkeby Test Network from faucet.rinkeby.io and follow the on-page instructions.

Borrowing fake/simulation Ether from faucet.rinkeby.io using a Twitter URL as authentication

If you choose to create a dummy DAO using dummy Ether, you will need to switch your MetaMask network from the Ethereum Mainnet to the Rinkeby Test Network. You can do this by clicking on the top dropdown menu (which is set to the Ethereum Mainnet by default), click on "Show/hide networks", and then toggle the "On" switch. From the original dropdown menu, you will now be able to select the Rinkeby Test Network.

After connecting your wallet to Aragon, you'll be asked to choose from a selection of pre-configured organizational templates, including **Company** (transferrable tokens and stake-weighted voting), **Membership** (transferrable tokens and one-member-one-vote), **Reputation** (non-transferable tokens and reputation-weight voting), **Open Enterprise** (apps for project planning and management), **Dandelion** (high rotation amongst contributors), and **Fundraising** (crowdfunding).

Template	Overview	Included Apps
Company	Transferrable tokens and stake-weighted voting	Voting, Tokens, Finance
Membership	Transferrable tokens and one-member-one-vote	Voting, Tokens, Finance
Reputation	Non-transferrable tokens and reputation-weighted voting	Voting, Tokens, Finance
Open Enterprise	Apps for project planning and management	Voting, Tokens, Finance, Address Book, Allocations, Dot Voting, Projects, Rewards
Dandelion	For DAOs with high rotation among contributors	Voting, Tokens, Finance, Time Lock, Redemptions, Token Request
Fundraising	Apps tailored for crowdfunding	Fundraising, Finance, Tokens, Voting

Overview of Aragon Client DAO templates

Follow the prompts to configure your chosen template and set thresholds for votes and vote duration, select a token name and symbol, and claim a name for your DAO. Note that the name of the DAO and token cannot be changed once they are confirmed.

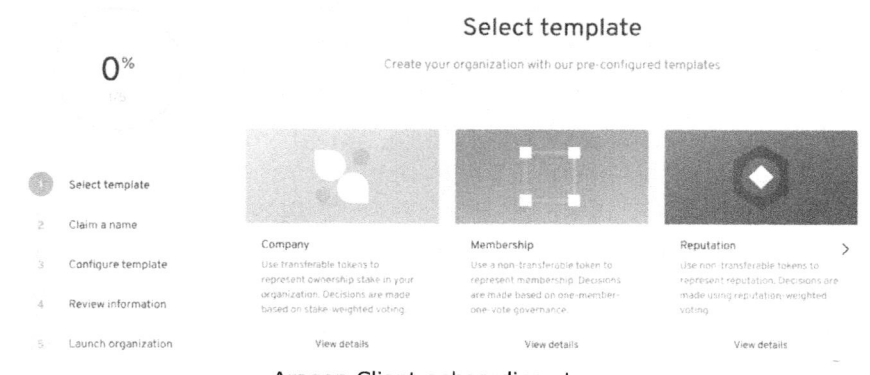

Aragon Client onboarding stage

After completing the onboarding process, you will have immediate access to the Aragon Client. From this dashboard, you can manage your DAO, including apps for adding members and assigning token holders, creating and setting rules for votes, managing finances, setting member rewards, and managing projects.

79

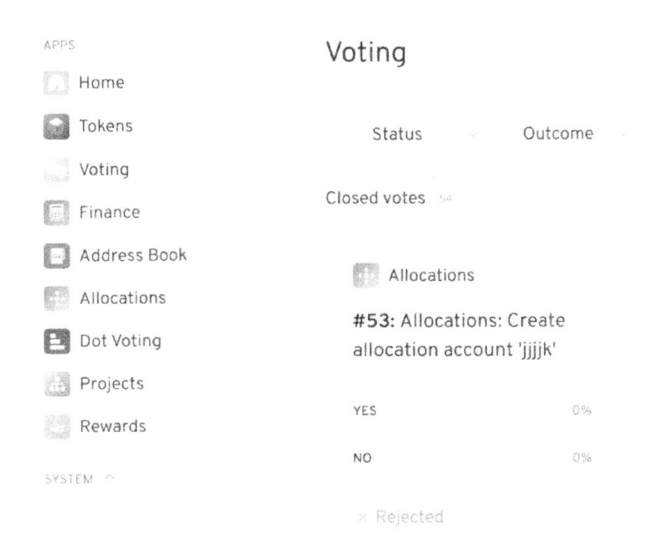

Aragon dashboard and apps

If you combine Aragon Client with a chat application such as Telegram or Discord, you will have the basic infrastructure needed to start building a new decentralized organization.

It's useful to know that while all-in-one tooling solutions such as Aragon Client, Colony, and Moloch are useful for new DAOs with a low or moderate level of technical know-how, most of the larger and established DAOs use a combination of focused tools such as Snapshot, POAPs (proof of attendance protocol), and Gnosis Safe, as covered in the next chapter.[28]

To learn more and see what tools other DAOs are using, you can review their stack at deepdao.io. There, you will find a leaderboard of popular DAOs including information about their platform tool(s), member numbers, token value, and voter participation rate. Uniswap and Compound, for example, operate on the Compound Governance platform, whereas Lido is running on Aragon, Aave on Snapshot, and BitDAO on Gnosis Safe and Snapshot.

---

[28] "DAOs: The New Coordination Frontier", *Gitcoin and BanklessDAO*, September 2021 Edition.

Name	Platform	USD Value ↓	Total In	Total Out	Members	Proposals	Voters	Voter Participation
Uniswap	Compound Governance	3,219,159,568.72	6,440,478,988.38	3,221,319,425.98	275,652	8	1,204	0.4
BitDAO	Gnosis Safe / Snapshot	2,723,875,707.53	2,736,940,909.09	203,742,111.94	10,000	5	25	0.3
Lido	Aragon	739,924,554.23	1,665,013,108.46	868,176,517.80	0	46	397	0.0
Compound	Compound Governance	683,986,239.93	1,503,676,421.97	819,689,980.17	174,329	79	1,025	0.6
Radicle	Compound Governance	601,883,055.95	659,310,212.70	57,427,156.75	5,597	4	60	1.1
Aave	Snapshot	541,258,352.59	795,987,650.98	254,729,298.40	11,212	77	13,929	100.0
Olympus DAO	Gnosis Safe / Snapshot	412,959,153.94	2,687,416,973.43	2,274,516,484.22	8,328	171	7,716	92.7
ENS	Snapshot	230,698,820.78	275,762,047.68	92,312,051.57	10,000	8	85,319	100.0
Maker Dao	Independent	208,494,746.13	943,615,774.54	735,121,028.41	82,614	–	–	–

Leaderboard of popular DAOs on deepdao.io, January 2022

9

DAO TOOLS

As DAOs mature as an entity for commerce and online activity, there will be increased demand for related products and services. Similar to how companies interact as suppliers, customers, consultants, and service providers in the traditional economy, DAO's will rely on each other for tooling, services, and commerce as part of the DAO-to-DAO or intra-DAO economy.

Designed by parties who understand the inherent needs of decentralized organizations, these products and services can be delivered on the blockchain using smart contracts and interoperable web3-native technology. These tools help to reduce complexity and lessen the load on DAO members by automating asset management, monitoring key metrics and analysis, and tracking and rewarding contributions.

Despite the nascent status of DAOs, there are already useful tools providing functionality and convenience for many of the DAOs mentioned in this book. In this chapter, we will review some of the most prominent tools and their practical applications.

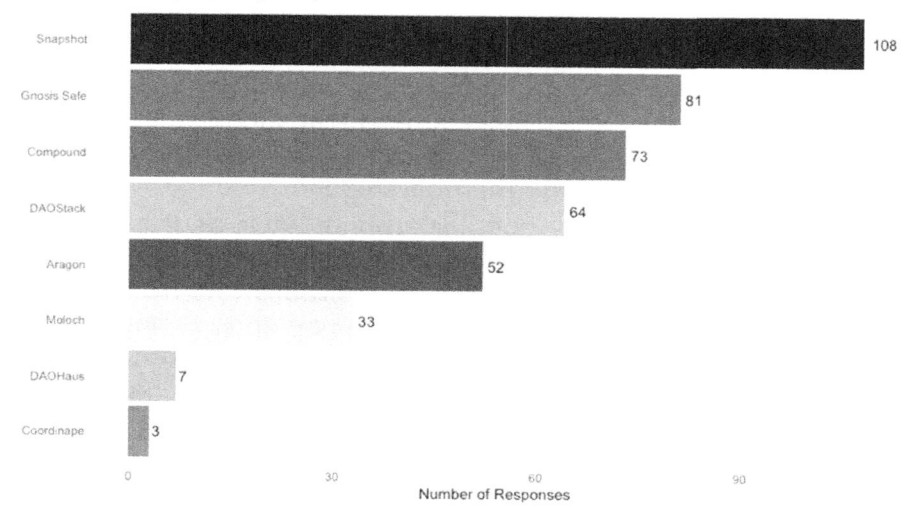

Is your DAO built upon any of these tools?
Total Survey Response (n = 256)

Tool	Number of Responses
Snapshot	108
Gnosis Safe	81
Compound	73
DAOStack	64
Aragon	52
Moloch	33
DAOHaus	7
Coordinape	3

Popular DAO tools, *DAOs: The New Coordination Frontier* 2021 report

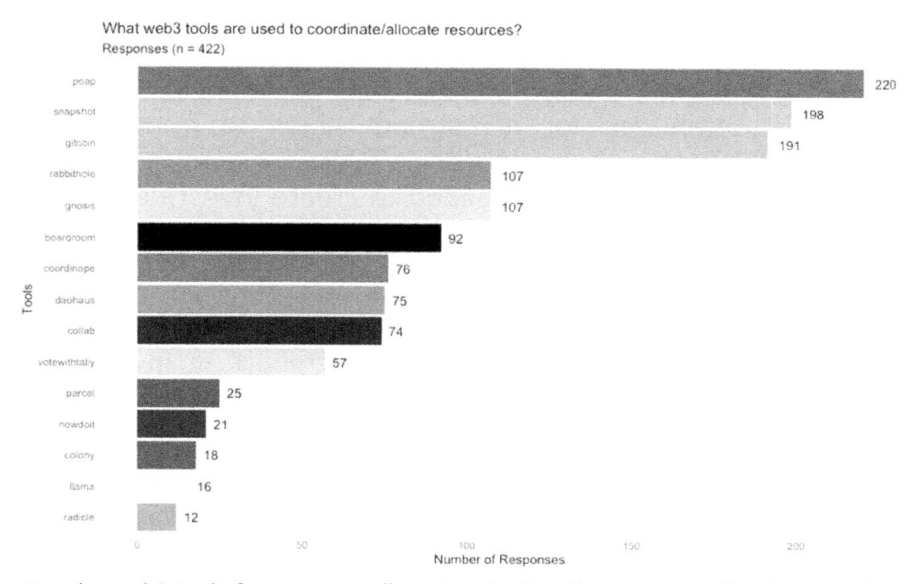

What web3 tools are used to coordinate/allocate resources?
Responses (n = 422)

Tool	Number of Responses
poap	220
snapshot	198
gitcoin	191
rabbithole	107
gnosis	107
boardroom	92
coordinape	76
daohaus	75
collab	74
votewithtally	57
parcel	25
nowdoit	21
colony	18
llama	16
radicle	12

Popular web3 tools for resource allocation, *DAOs: The New Coordination Frontier* 2021 report

Treasury Management & Funding

Gnosis Safe | gnosis-safe.io

Gnosis Safe is a flexible and secure multi-signature wallet used for managing funds, assets, and transactions. For DAOs, Gnosis Safe offers a platform to run their treasury, delegate voting rights, and manage membership.

Gnosis Safe is especially popular among DAOs as it addresses the complex problem of managing shared ownership of funds. Using different policies, deposits and withdrawals from Gnosis Safe require confirmation from a pre-defined number of members, which prevents any single person from moving funds without authorization. A policy defines who has access to what part of the total amount of an organization's treasury or token supply, as well as when certain actions can take place. To illustrate, a policy could be set that only the director can make withdrawals or that sending funds requires signatures from multiple individuals in order to authorize the transaction.

Syndicate | syndicate.io

Syndicate provides a suite of Ethereum-based tools and legal document templates for investment clubs to operate and invest as DAOs.

The Syndicate platform is intended to create investment DAOs that are compliant with SEC investment club regulations, including tax compliance and fully disclosing members to comply with U.S. anti-money laundering and anti-terrorism rules. Other requirements include having no more than 99 members, active participation by all members in investment decisions, no transferability, no performance fees, and no public solicitations or public offerings. Also, unless all members are "accredited investors" or the DAO has a separate legal entity, then the DAO can only invest in NFTs and/or tokens and not off-chain investment categories.

The Syndicate suite includes a digital wallet, governance token distribution, and smart contracts to manage their deposits, investment portfolio, reporting, and distributions. Syndicate also provides a dashboard for members to keep track of their stake, portfolio performance, and other key information.

Lastly, Syndicate has partnered with Latham & Watkins to generate and provide legal documents that can be easily shared, collected, and signed online.

Mirror | mirror.xyz/race

Mirror is a decentralized content platform for writers with cryptocurrency and other blockchain technology integrations. In this way, Mirror is similar to Medium.com but for web3. For DAOs, Mirror provides a decentralized platform to publish content and a useful tokenized crowdfunding feature that can be used for financing creative projects.

Parcel | parcel.money

Founded and based in India, Parcel is a treasury management protocol for DAOs. Compatible with Gnosis Safe, Parcel allows DAOs to easily track and send payments. This includes the ability to add or import CSVs for payee details, run payrolls or pay a group in Ether or ERC-20 tokens as well as schedule automated recurring payouts.

Other treasury services include yield optimization and strategic asset management that includes custom strategies for treasury diversification and token buybacks.

Boardroom | boardroom.info

Boardroom provides a suite of services for DAOs including governance and voting features, discussion and proposal platforms, and treasury management services that are compatible with Gnosis Safe.

Governance Management

Snapshot | snapshot.org

Snapshot.org is an off-chain and gasless polling platform. According to the *DAOs: The New Coordination Frontier* 2021 report, Snapshot was the top tool used by DAOs and the second most popular web3 tool for DAO resource coordination.

Snapshot enables DAO members to vote on open proposals using an easy-to-use voting dashboard. While the information on Snapshot can be accessed by anyone with a link to the snapshot, only token holders have the power to vote. Voting rules are allocated at the time of the snapshot's proposal, which means that you need to own a given token at the time of the proposal's creation in order to vote. Voting power is also typically weighted based on the quantity or special value of tokens a member holds.

While you will need to log in to Snapshot using your digital wallet (e.g. MetaMask wallet), all voting takes place off-chain, which means there are no fees required to cast a vote.

Tally | withtally.com

Tally provides a governance dashboard for DAOs to track on-chain voting history across different protocols including Gitcoin, Uniswap, and Compound. Tally offers similar features as Snapshot such as the ability to add proposals and cast votes on others' proposals—except that the voting takes place on the blockchain, which is not the case with Snapshot.

Sybil | sybil.org

Sybil is another on-chain governance system but also supports vote delegation and integrates with a range of DeFi protocols including Uniswap, Compound, and Aave.

Sybil works by mapping on-chain addresses to social identities (currently based on Twitter profiles but will expand to GitHub soon) in order to maintain a list of DAO members. Identities are valid across platforms, which means that members can sign into multiple web3 platforms after completing one-time verification.

Through Sybil, verified DAO members have the ability to stand as a delegate or delegate their vote(s) to others, which supports representative leadership on highly technical decisions.

Beyond vote delegation, Sybil's mapping of on-chain addresses to social identities supports gamified leaderboards and Ethereum-based messaging.

Communication & Collaboration

Discourse | discourse.org

Discourse is an online forum service that allows users to discuss and collaborate on topics related to DAOs (particularly in regards to governance proposals) and other blockchain-based projects.

On Discourse, users can share ideas and feedback about specific DAO projects, as well as connect with others who are interested in this space. This is an important resource for anyone looking to learn more about DAOs and specific projects.

Collab.land | collab.land

Powered on the Ethereum blockchain, Collab.land uses smart contracts to automate project management tasks and ensure that all stakeholders are fairly compensated for their contributions. Collab.land allows DAO members to create and manage projects collaboratively, including bots providing token-gated access and tipping for community chat groups.

One of the key benefits of Collab.land is it eliminates the need for trust between collaborators. All interactions are mediated by the blockchain, which ensures that agreements are enforced and mistakes are unlikely to occur. This makes Collab.land ideal for projects that require a high level of trust and collaboration, such as software development or scientific research.

Collab.land also offers a number of features that make it easier for members to collaborate effectively, including a task management system, discussion forum, and voting system. Users can also earn rewards for their contributions by participating in the DAO's governance system.

Contribution Management

Coordinape | coordinape.com

Marketed as the "Asana for DAOs", Coordinape enables DAOs to manage resources, tasks, and payroll across multiple teams, time zones, and pseudonymous identities.

Coordinape is popular among DAOs because of its "gamified consensus" tools that can be used to distribute compensation for projects, grants, and salaries to contributors. Integrating game elements and a peer-to-peer reward system, Coordinape lets DAO members collectively reward others' contributions.

This works by allocating tokens to all project contributors, who must then award those tokens to other contributors based on performance over a set time period called an "epoch". At the end of the epoch, each individual is rewarded proportionately based on the number of tokens they hold, which are converted into a financial reward released from the DAO's treasury.

The entire system is transparent. This means that participants can see how value and resources flow through the organization as well as who is tipping and supporting them! Naturally, there are potential limitations to this method, including unfair cooperation and short-term uncertainty over earnings potential. For one, a participant has no idea how much they will earn when they sign up for a project, and two, their reimbursement is based on the subjective opinion of their peers, who may have a secret pact to reward certain members.

POAP | poap.xyz

Marketed as "bookmarks of your life", POAPs (Proof of Attendance Protocol) are digital mementos on the Ethereum blockchain. Governed by poap.xyz, POAPs are linked to a person's Ethereum address rather than their real identity, such as a passport or email address. In effect, each POAP is a reward or a gift from an issuer to a collector to acknowledge non-material contributions. By minting these memories on the blockchain, collectors can build a record of their past experiences and unlock unique benefits, including financial rewards and future utility (i.e. access to events). For the collector, POAPs also provide digital proof that they attended or participated in an event or activity.

In the context of DAOs, this might mean a POAP reward for members who contribute in the form of participation, energy, donation, time, or another action that can be redeemed for an NFT drop or access to an offline DAO event.

SourceCred | sourcecred.io

SourceCred is an open-source tool used by DAOs to track community participation and reward value creation among active members based on a special metric called "Cred".

Using an algorithm to determine how much value a contribution or contributor brought to a project as a whole, Cred makes the labor of individuals more visible and rewardable as they work on a project or within a community. The algorithm employs what are called "weights", which are a set of rules—set by the DAO—stating which types of contributions are worth what amounts of Cred. Cred is also non-transferable and cannot be bought or sold.

Cred, for example, is mapped from the contribution to all the members and other contributions that supported it. The concept borrows from node graph theory, which shows connections between nodes (individuals) and lines/edges (connections), with more edges generating more potential value.

Onboarding

Rabbithole | rabbithole.gg

Rabbithole is an educational tool that allows users with a crypto wallet to discover and use decentralized apps (DApps), protocols, or crypto platforms in return for cryptocurrency rewards. DAOs can also use Rabbithole's proof-of-use and learn-to-earn features to distribute tokens to members as a reward.

The platform includes tutorials on topics including DeFi, NFTs, voting, and token swapping as well as quests that allow users to demonstrate their knowledge of specific topics. A quest, for example, might lead the user through a two-step process to register an ENS domain or vote on a Snapshot governance proposal.

For DAOs, these quests incentivize the onboarding phase for new members, reinforce participation, and help to retain member attention.

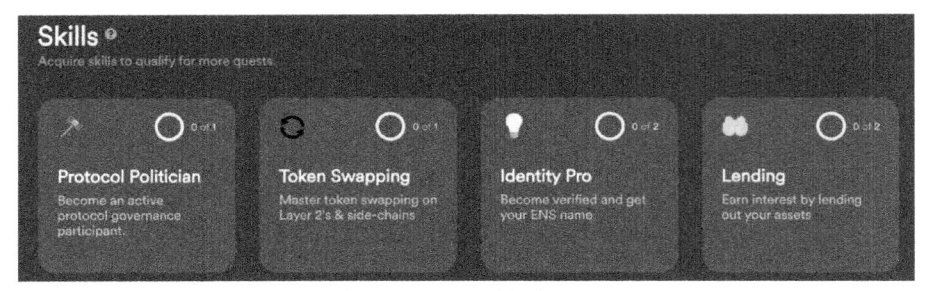

Skill quests on Rabbithole.gg

10

THE FUTURE OF DAOS

The future for DAOs looks bright, and if designed right, they could help usher in a new period of accelerated democracy and decentralized decision-making on the blockchain. This technology, including smart contracts, non-fungible tokens, and cryptocurrencies, unlocks new ways of collaboration, coordination, production, and compensation that pave the way for a transfer of value from centralized organizations to decentralized ones.

For individuals, DAOs offer flexibility and autonomy, and in the future, switching jobs may be as simple as transferring tokens and introducing yourself in a new group chat. For retirees, laid-off workers, or solopreneurs who don't want to work alone for the rest of their lives, DAOs also offer a path to reconnect with a team environment, vibe with like-minded people, and participate in meaningful work. It will also become more common to build a record of past performance or a digital resume under a psuedonoym, which unlike anoymonity, can accumulate reputation and relationships over time. In fact, a career under your new pseudonym might become more successful renown than your real name.

Eventually, once DAOs become a more reliable source of income, working for a traditional company—with various forms of lock-in—will likely lose appeal as the default option for many people. Already in the traditional labor market, we are witnessing the unbundling of employment where the individual can operate as an independent unit in the gig and creator economy. Without the constraints of working at a single company under a fixed job description, individuals are better positioned to follow their interests, collaborate on multiple projects, work when they want, and pursue a more fluid and spontaneous career path.

As more people become aware of the benefits of DAOs, and as the technology continues to evolve, we can expect to see new waves of DAOs emerge. According to Jake and Stake, writing for the BanklessDAO Substack, "DAOs will follow similar trends as the internet: there will be a few very large DAOs and there will be a long-tail of smaller DAOs."[29] This prediction is based on the hypothesis that highly mobile individuals will spend most of their time with communities that resonate the most, which will inevitably lead to active participation in the more obscure DAOs that make up the long-tail. A limited number of DAOs, meanwhile, will attract a large number of members courtesy of their brand name and monopoly on public recognition.

Over the coming years, many types of offline and online organizations will also be recast as DAOs, including businesses, charities, social networks, media outlets, clubs, investment groups, unions, political groups, scientific research units, and sporting clubs. This will ultimately lead to a more decentralized and democratic world where organizations are more responsive and aligned to the needs of their members and stakeholders.

Traditional political parties, in particular, are prime candidates to organize under a DAO structure. As with philanthropic DAOs, the blockchain offers an ideal platform for community building, collecting ideas, and raising public funds. Greater transparency also makes it easier for voters to know who is supporting the party and make informed decisions. Legacy political parties may not be the first movers, but new DAOs will one day form to provide this social layer and catalyst for political and institutional change.

With that said, there are still issues that need to be addressed before DAOs can be fully integrated into the traditional economy. This includes security issues related to anonymity, fiat on-ramps, and creating robust code with proper safeguards. In addition, centralized leadership and professional managers might still be necessary when it comes to dealing with external third parties where individual influence and negotiation skills come are needed.

---

[29] Jake and Stake, "Beginnings of the In-DAO-strial Revolution", *BanklessDAO*, December 2021.

At present, most of the collaboration is DAO-to-DAO and isolated from the traditional economy. However, once existing organizations and web2 platforms like Twitter and PayPal adopt web3 practices, and DAOs find new ways to manage fiat currency and gain legal recognition, it's possible that DAOs could become more mainstream and not just the nascent shadow economy it is today.

Lastly, it's responsible to acknowledge that the future of DAOs is, in some places, grossly over-romanticized. The notion that you can get rich and improve the world in one clean stroke overlooks the unique shortcomings that come with this new form of group coordination, including those still being discovered. Pioneering the future isn't easy, and there are many obstacles that need to be addressed before DAOs reach their full potential and contributors are faily compensated for their work. This includes the lack of standardization, automation, and regulatory clarity around how DAOs operate as well as the trade-off between open and gated access that raises problems with inequality. Moreover, there are questions over how DAOs should develop and scale effectively while also balancing security and avoiding voting apathy. While we can't expect every DAO to remain relevant forever, it's important that DAOs build long-term incentives to promote a sense of community and retain talent that is both highly mobile and independent in nature.

As we play out the first innings, it's equally challenging to predict the long-term impact and longevity of individual DAOs. Time will show that it's easier to start a DAO than it is to actually maintain that movement and there's a fine line to keeping contributors active and loyal. With the soaring valuations of DeFi DAOs, tokens, and other assets, the true mantle and staying power of individual DAOs will also be tested when the current cycle bursts and these organizations are forced to survive during lower levels of interest, media attention, and asset valuations.

What's more, not all DAO's are designed to last forever. DAOs such as the FreeRossDAO, whose mission is to free the alleged Silk Road founder Ross Ulbricht from jail, may not need to continue if the DAO's mission is achieved. For this type of single-case mission, a DAO should be allowed to fold or reincarnate and release or repurpose members' time, energy, and resources, such as merging with another DAO with similar goals. An example of this could be the FreeRossDAO later merging with the AssangeDAO, which was created to finance legal fees and support WikiLeaks founder Julian Assange.

THANK YOU

Thank you for reading this short primer on decentralized autonomous organizations. I enjoyed composing this guide and I hope you are inspired to continue the journey in exploring the many new opportunities that DAOs offer now and into the future. If you would like to continue your journey down the web3 rabbit hole, then you may also like to read my other book: **The Metaverse: Prepare Now for the Next Big Thing**.

As we have explored, DAOs provide a new and flexible way to earn an income and serve a purpose in both the digital world and web3 era. In addition, by incorporating as a DAO, groups of like-minded individuals have the potential to facilitate new types of collaborative work, income creation, and social interactions that we have not yet seen on such a global scale. While DAOs are not for everyone, they offer considerable freedom and autonomy for self-starters, and like most things, value usually lies at the fringes.

Aside from directly participating in DAOs, there will be many opportunities to serve these organizations with specific software-as-a-service offerings, similar to those mentioned in this book, as well as third-party lawyers, artists, and developers that will feed into the DAO economy.

To choose a DAO to work or invest in, you can find numerous aggregators to simplify the selection process including deepdao.io and the Live DAO Directory on Notion. Bear in mind that each DAO is different, and you will need to research how members collaborate, where to propose ideas, and how progress is ultimately made. In addition, many DAOs provide an option to explore the discussion boards and check out the general vibe without purchasing native tokens. Even after joining a DAO, you will still need to be in constant "learning mode" in order to keep up with the fast pace of activity, including how to use different software tools and technology.

Eventually, you may even like to forge a new movement by launching a DAO. If you have an innate desire to contribute to something larger than yourself, and, even beyond profit, then creating a DAO could be a life-changing opportunity. Indeed, I look forward to hearing what readers achieve through this new paradigm shift in how groups collaborate.

Finally, I would like to thank the Gitcoin and BanklessDAO report referenced throughout this book, which provided the most comprehensive survey of the DAO landscape at the time of writing. I would also like to thank and acknowledge other valuable sources of information in researching this book including Cooper Turley, the BanklessDAO, Real Vision and founder Raoul Pal, Tarun Chutri, Andrew Bull, Gaby Goldberg, Sven Rika, Kevin Rose and the Modern Finance podcast, The Defiant YouTube channel, Elliot Couvat, and the author of *Token Economy*, Shermin Voshmgir.

For inquiries, suggestions, or expressions of interest to cooperate, please contact me at: terrywinters@protonmail.com

Or get to know me on Twitter: terrywinters07

APPENDIX

Discord

As an instant messaging and digital distribution platform, Discord is one of the primary communication hubs for DAOs and blockchain projects, currently followed in second by Telegram.

You can use Discord to communicate via voice call, video call, instant messaging, as well as send files in private chats and form communities called "servers". Most of the major DAOs have a Discord channel as well as a series of servers for hosting targeted conversations, including onboarding for new users and other special interest servers. These servers are a great source of information and provide a valuable place to ask questions.

Naturally, you should always exercise vigilance in order to avoid potential scams shared in Discord servers, including suspicious external links, and never disclose information that might jeopardize the security of your digital wallet or other private property.

Digital Wallet

Whether it's voting on a governance proposal, receiving funds for work contributed to a DAO, or buying tokens to join, at some stage you will need to install a digital browser-based wallet. Additionally, you will need a digital wallet in order to log into online DAO platforms.

Contrary to popular belief, a digital wallet in the context of cryptocurrency and tokens does not directly store those assets as they belong on the blockchain. Instead, the digital wallet holds the public-private key associated with your blockchain address, which provides access to your assets recorded on the blockchain. The wallet also provides access to a record of all your past transactions.

At the time of writing, the most common wallet for interacting with Ethereum-based platforms is a browser extension wallet called MetaMask. Using the MetaMask wallet, you will be able to send and receive Ethereum-based coins including Ether

(ETH), FWB (Friends with Benefits), and OHM (Olympus DAO), as well as log into Ethereum-based DAOs.

MetaMask is available with Google Chrome, Firefox, Brave, and Edge browsers. To download MetaMask, first go to metamask.io or your browser store, such as the Chrome Store, and download the official MetaMask extension. From there, follow the wallet setup instructions.

When you first install and open MetaMask, it will issue you a randomly generated 12-word seed phrase. It's crucial that you store those 12 words somewhere safe. This information has the potential to unlock the full contents of your wallet, so it's very important that you make sure this seed phrase is safe and secure. If anything ever happens to your computer or your MetaMask account, as long as you have your 12-word seed phrase, there is no need to worry, as all your account details and funds will be recoverable.

It's recommended that you write down and store the seed phrase in a safe place (most people recommend something like a fireproof safe) and not save the seed phrase to a digital device, which may be susceptible to hacking.

Next, add MetaMask to your browser tab in the top-right if it has not appeared there automatically.

Look for the fox icon in your browser extension section or add it by clicking on the three dots on the right

When you first log in to MetaMask, you will be asked whether you want MetaMask to act as your default browser for accessing DApps (decentralized applications or programs that exist and run on a blockchain or peer-to-peer network). Selecting "Yes" means that every time you click on a link requesting access to your digital wallet, it will open via MetaMask and you can log in without ever having to take any extra signup steps. This essentially makes using DApps as easy as using normal mobile apps on your smartphone.

In terms of security, it's important to recognize that MetaMask is an online wallet, which is exposed to more potential security risks than hardware wallets and other forms of cold storage for storing your crypto holdings. Phishing attacks (fraudulent communications that appear to come from a reputable source) are one of the common risks facing MetaMask wallet holders.

Holding the private keys to your coins and tokens in your MetaMask is therefore not recommended for long-term storage. Please conduct your own research in order to best secure your digital funds.

Buying Tokens

To acquire tokens, you can buy on a centralized cryptocurrency exchange such as Coinbase, Kraken, Binance, and Gemini, or from a decentralized exchange such as Sushiswap and Uniswap to purchase DAO tokens including FWB and OHM.

To send tokens to your MetaMask wallet from a centralized exchange, you will need to enter your wallet's ENS (Ethereum name service) address, which represents your Ethereum account and which also acts as your cross-platform web3 username and profile. By default, the ENS domain consists of a 42-character hexadecimal address that looks something like this: 0x8155e981BCeCDEB4f2b77db16d49Dbd2E6d18E62

Note that you can purchase your own custom ENS domain at https://ens.domains for as low as 0.001 ETH (5 USD as of late 2021) per year plus gas fees, which for the time being, far exceeds the cost of the actual ENS domain. Also note that you can only have one primary ENS domain per Ethereum account, which you can change at any time. This means, that while you can have two ENS domains, only one ENS domain can be linked to your Ethereum wallet at one time, and any other domains are inactive unless they are linked to another Ethereum wallet that you are using. Also, keep in mind that you can buy and sell ENS domains on secondary markets including OpenSea.

Lastly, in terms of selecting a cryptocurrency exchange to purchase tokens, you will need to factor in what coins the exchange offers (i.e. as of 2021 Coinbase does not offer OHM and FWB), eligibility requirements based on what country you reside in and/or your tax location, and whether you are eligible to wire/transfer fiat (i.e. USD, GBP, AUD) to an exchange to purchase cryptocurrencies. In general, you want to avoid buying coins using a credit card due to the higher transaction fees. You will also need to factor in exchange fees based on your preferred payment method and other policies such as security and overall ease of use.

FURTHER RESOURCES

DAOs: The New Coordination Frontier
Published by Gitcoin and BanklessDAO in September 2021

Token Economy: How the Web3 reinvents the Internet, Second Edition
Published by Token Kitchen in 2021 and authored by Shermin Voshmgir

What is a DAO? The Defiant Guide
Published by The Defiant channel on YouTube in 2021

coopahtroopa.mirror.xyz
Cooper Turley's personal content site, where he writes about DAOs and other crypto trends.

Podcasts of Note
Bankless, Ryan Sean Adams and David Hoffman
Modern Finance, Kevin Rose
The Delphi Podcast, Tom Shaughnessy
Real Vision Crypto
Hello Metaverse, Annie Zhang

FREQUENTLY ASKED QUESTIONS

Where can I purchase governance tokens for a DAO I want to join?

For large-cap DeFi DAOs and some service-side DAOs including Aragon, you can purchase tokens on a centralized exchange platform such as Coinbase, Binance, and Gemini. Most DAO tokens, though, are traded on decentralized exchanges including SushiSwap and Uniswap. To purchase governance tokens on a decentralized exchange, you will first need to purchase another token such as Ether on a centralized exchange, associate those tokens with a digital wallet (i.e. MetaMask wallet), and then connect your digital wallet to the decentralized exchange to initiate a swap (i.e. Ether for the native DAO token). The process, however, will vary for each DAO, so it's crucial to check the DAO's website, Discord, or onboarding pack for instructions regarding the most efficient way to buy governance tokens.

Do I have to pay to join a DAO?

While entry requirements will vary, most DAOs follow a pay-to-participate model. Newly established DAOs or DAOs that ask members to contribute through non-financial means (i.e. commit code or write a news article) are more likely to offer unpaid entry into their communities. Some DAOs, including BanklessDAO, also provide a guest pass system with read-only Discord channels that enable you to observe the DAO before making a financial commitment.

Do I need to pay tax on my DAO earnings?

Tax obligations will vary from country to country. Some DAO participants report foregoing the need to report tokens received in lieu of their contributions given that cryptocurrency is not taxed in their country of residence. To learn more about your tax obligations, you will need to consult a professional in your local tax jurisdiction or potentially consider moving to a location that is more friendly to reporting cryptocurrency-based income.

Do I need to be a developer or crypto expert to join a DAO?

DAOs accept contributions and membership from nondevelopers, including many of the same professional roles found in a traditional organization. Even highly technical and developer-orientated DAOs such as Gitcoin need a diverse membership including contributors without a computer science major.

Common roles in a DAO include recruiter, promoter, writer, memester, administrator, product manager, event manager, marketer, designer, and translator. This list shows that you don't need to be a crypto expert to participate and add value. However, you will need a basic level of crypto and web3 literacy to set up a digital wallet and vote on blockchain-based platforms.

Printed in Great Britain
by Amazon